RED SPANISH NOTEBOOK

The First Six Months of the Revolution and the Civil War

by
Mary Low
and
Juan Breá

with a new introduction by
E. Granell

CITY LIGHTS BOOKS
San Francisco

Introduction translated by Nancy J. Peters and Pamela Mosher

Thanks to Stephen Schwartz for loan of cover photos of
Mary Low & Juan Breá

The first edition of this book was published by
Martin Secker and Warburg, Ltd., London, 1937.

Library of Congress Cataloging in Publication Data
Low, Mary.
    Red Spanish notebook.
    Reprint of the 1937 ed. published by Secker
and Warburg, London.
    1. Spain—History—Civil War, 1936-1939—
Personal narratives.   2. Low, Mary.   3. Breá,
Juan.   I. Breá, Juan, joint author.   II. Title.
DP269.9.L69   1979   946.081   79-11919
ISBN 0-87286-132-5

CITY LIGHTS BOOKS are edited by Lawrence Ferlinghetti &
Nancy J. Peters and published at the City Lights Bookstore,
261 Columbus Avenue, San Francisco, California 94133.

A LIVING VISION OF THE REVOLUTION

The present edition of *Red Spanish Notebook* by Mary Low and Juan Breá, fills an enormous lacuna in the formidable bibliography of the civil war in Spain (1936-1939), which today includes some 20,000 books and nearly two million documents of all kinds. In this immensity of printed paper, reflecting the far-reaching importance of the revolution, this book shines like an exceptional jewel. Not only in being among those which began the historic recording of events, but because its eighteen chronicles offer an incomparably faithful vision of days which were believed would change the face of the earth.

Still very young, both authors fought in the POUM militias during the first months of the revolutionary thrust. They experienced with their comrades-in-arms the urgent anxiety of the rear guard, and with the militias the danger of the battle front. They passionately discussed problems of burning importance with socialists, anarchists and liberals. They shared their vicissitudes, anguish and hopes with peasants, workers and people in the militias, with bureaucrats and journalists, technicians, politicians, poets and professionals. Reading this book conveys a sense of fervent exigency which never deviates from what impelled personal intervention in the events it relates.

Mary Low and Juan Breá totally immersed themselves in the sweeping currents that incited the people against the fascist rebellion. For Mary Low and Juan Breá, their rifles were like two bold pen strokes, joined with many others, underlining the conviction that the will to win and victory were synonymous terms. And they were right to believe it. Like so many others, like ourselves, they were certain that they possessed the technical instrument, derived from scientific theories, whose mechanism would enable traditional society to be transformed into another, socialist one.

The revolution divided Spain, and all humanity, into two factions. Fighting on one side were the precariously armed, improvised militias of the socialist ideal. The powerful armies of the modern fascist states reinforced Franco on the other side. The quantitative and qualitative difference in armaments and the degree of military preparation of both sides gave a crushing advantage to the Francoists. Years before, another great social conflagration had broken out in Russia, but the hopeful days of that red dawn—which in the words of John Reed—shook the world, were mere cinders when the first shots of the Spanish revolution were fired. The Bolshevik conquest of power had already been converted, under Stalin, into the world's most terrible totalitarian state which is why it served as a model, in part, for Mussolini and Hitler.

The Russian revolution and the Spanish were very different. The enemy of the Russian people was tsarism, greatly weakened by the reverses of the war of 1914-1918. For this reason, "when in October some hundreds of soldiers attacked the strongholds of Tsarist power in Petrograd, they encountered little resistance. . . . Trotsky commented many years later: 'the residents slept tranquilly and did not know that within a few minutes a new power would be substituted for the old.' Lenin had corroborated it: 'It was easy to begin the revolution in a similar country; it turned out to be simpler than lifting a pen.'*"[1] In Spain everybody was wide awake, each one with a pen, as the chronicles of Low and Breá testify. Unfortunately the gigantic repressive apparatus in Moscow was not asleep either; while it physically destroyed the Bolshevik old guard at home, instead of troops, it sent hordes of police and NKVD torturers to Spain.

In 1936 Spain was far ahead of Russia in 1917 in revolutionary consciousness and in workers' organization. Spain was much more highly industrialized. The UGT (Unión General de Trabajadores) and the Socialist Party together had a million and a half adherents. The CNT (Confederación Nacional del Trabajo) with a libertarian orientation and the anarchists accounted for as many more. The Communist Party had 50,000 members at the outbreak of the revolution,

---

* In the idiom "lifting a feather," the Spanish *pluma* also means pen. These words are synonyms in Russian too.

and no prestige. The POUM with 10,000 members and a union organization important only in Catalonia, was to increase its ranks and extend its influence throughout the entire national territory.

The revolution expanded from the first moment with a force not to be contained. Its scope was much deeper and wider than that of the Russian Revolution. The existence of large workers' organizations with solid revolutionary experience would seem to ensure the establishment of a genuinely democratic socialist system; the power of the bourgeois Republican government was merely nominal and legal. The entire compass of the loyal zone—so called in opposition to the rebels—was dominated by the workers and peasant committees of the two great central unions. A large number of agrarian and industrial communes immediately spread throughout the whole country.[2] The workers were owners of the means of production, distribution, administration and arms.

In Spain the enemy was international fascism which the Russians were not acquainted with. But the militias could not direct their efforts to fighting only against fascism entrenched on the other side of the line of fire. If that were not enough, they had to defend themselves from the mortal blows of the Stalinists in the rear guard as well as in their own trenches. This situation greatly obstructed the consolidation of the revolutionary conquests. The CP grew astronomically, allied with the bourgeois parties through the Popular Front built by Stalin for this purpose and attracted to itself extensive sections of the petty bourgeoisie—and also numerous secret fascists. Stalin gave the order to exterminate the Trotskyists—which were all the individuals & organizations not Stalinist. And in exchange he consented to send some arms, limited in number and outmoded models, to Spain on the condition that they be destined for the Communist military formations. The Republican government paid for this materiel with 460.5 tons of pure gold, with a nominal value of 518 million dollars at that time. Never have bombs and guns been sold, least of all to proletarian brothers, at such an exorbitant price!

The POUM was the most revolutionary party, and the most in disfavor in the counterrevolutionary calculations of Stalin. For this reason many revolutionaries like Mary Low and Juan Brea, like Benjamin Péret, George Orwell, Landau, Etchébehère and many more joined its ranks. And that is why Stalinism unleashed all its fury against the POUM. The POUM was not a Trotskyist party; one of its leaders Andrés Nin had lived in Russia for many years and was a personal friend of Trotsky, but he was in disagreement with many viewpoints of the greater organizer of the Red Army, — with Lenin, the major leader of the October revolution. Trotskyism, as we know, is the brand with which Stalinism tattooes all its dissidents.

At the end of 1936 the CP was very strong, and thanks to Russian blackmail, its forces had more arms than the rest of the anti-fascist sectors. With its allies in the Popular Front the Communists succeeded in changing the direction of the revolution. The militias were eliminated. A Popular Army was created. The watchword was imposed—defend the whole (bourgeois) Republic and win the war first, leaving the revolution—for later. The POUM, the CNT and the left socialists protested. But more powerful than the protests were the armaments and the agents of the NKVD, who launched a violent campaign of extermination against the POUM, which was immediately extended to the anarchists and the left socialists. Just as in Moscow, the trials came later. The Poum leaders were jailed; others chased or killed, as its greatest figures Nin and Maurín. Maurín had been thrown into an obscure Francoist prison and saved from the firing squad because he wasn't recognized until very late. Nin was detained by the NKVD, led to Alcalá de Henares, bestially tortured, and when Orloff* failed to compel him to tell lies, was assassinated. Many Poumists suffered the same fate. And also a great number of socialists and anarchists. Among the latter, their great leader Durruti died on the Madrid front. Mika Etchébehère did not die, as Low and

---

* Alexander Orloff, chief of NKVD in Spain.

Breá thought. She lives in Paris and wrote a book on the POUM column first commanded by her husband Hipolito on the Sigüenza front, and later by herself on the Madrid front: *Mi propia guerra de España*.[3] Julio (Fernandez Granell), my brother, was Chief of Operations of an anarchist brigade under Mera and lives in Venezuela. Other names mentioned in *Red Spanish Notebook* are Molins y Fábrega who died a few years ago in Mexico; Andrade, Arquer, Gironella, Julian and Luisa Gorkin, Bonet and Rovira went into exile in France. Many friends were assassinated; some by the fascist repression, others by the Stalinist terror, and hundreds fell on the fronts during the war.

Let us finally remember with sadness that the POUM was fiercely fought by the great revolutionary and Red Army organizer Leon Trotsky, so admired for his personal acts and his writings. Trotsky suffered from a complete misunderstanding of the Spanish revolution. The epic exaltation of the Russian achievement which he carried to an extreme—perhaps unconsciously motivated by his tremendous opposition to Stalinism and by the nostalgia of his long exile—idealizing it out of proportion, led him to convert into rigid dogmas the vital lessons which he himself had been able to extract from a historic moment, unduplicatable in Spain or anywhere else. Because they did not adjust themselves to his inflexible schema, he accused the leaders of the POUM of being traitors and counterrevolutionaries.* In the heat of combatting Stalinism, the great revolutionary ended up infected by that movement's most corrosive moral evil, calumny. This, and his conceptual rigidity of later years, is the only food which nourishes today's Trotskyism, which repeats to the point of obsession the same blind analysis of the revolution, an analysis which will never apply.

The fact is that manuals for preparing revolutions do not exist as do cookbooks for preparing meals. Culinary errors can result in indigestion. Bolshevik-Leninist errors led revolutionaries into terrible massacres. It is necessary to begin

---

* After Nin's assassination, Trotsky wrote about his revolutionary behavior and personal honesty.

again from zero and entirely remake all revolutionary theory. As for how to make socialist revolutions, we currently have in our possession only an encyclopedia of ignorance. In addition to the confusion produced by the defeat of the Russian and Spanish revolutions, the face of the present world has become so intricately complex, and frequently appears so arbitrary, that the works of Ionesco look like a new *Discours de la Mèthode* when faced with the absurd grimaces of contemporary daily life.

—E. Granell

1. Ignacio Iglesias, *Trotsky et la Révolution Espagnole*. Editions du Monde, Genève, 1974, p. 17.
2. Sam Dolgoff, *The Anarchist Collectives. Workers' Self-management in the Spanish Revolution, 1936-1939*. Free Life Editions. New York, 1974. An excellent study on this subject.
3. Mika Etchébehère, *Ma Guerre d'Espagne à Moi. Une Femme à la tête d'une Colonne au Combat*. Denöel, Paris, 1975.

CONTENTS

CONTENTS

RED SPANISH NOTEBOOK

I

JOURNEY THERE
(*Narrative by Mary Low*)

JULY 19TH, 1936, WITH ITS WHOLE SURGE OF bravery, fine deeds and the violent foretaste of new life had already passed over Barcelona. The month was moving on the train of those days. The streets were untidy, streaked with dust and old paper, and the air was hot, eager and compressed. The excitement, the feeling of living again, of being reborn, that was what struck one most. Everything seemed about to come true.

We had come straight from the other side of Belgium to go to Barcelona, but there was no connection in the trains in Paris, and we had to spend the day. In Paris it was very early morning. We lingered about the station, uncertain what to do with ourselves. A curious, early smell, native to Paris, penetrated into the glass nave of the station and hung about under the vaulting. It was a mixture of warm croissants, fresh air, street washing and a flavour of gas. We had no money, and knapsacks on our backs.

The porters walked past where we stood, the
ends of their blue smocks frilling out round their
hips like ballet skirts below the tight elastic belts.
They made jokes. I only wanted to get to
Barcelona; their jokes irritated me, especially
because of the French sound of the words which
I heard as they walked past me talking.

The train with third class to Barcelona left
at night from the Gare d'Orsay. After we had
spent an idle day in the streets, we went across
the arch of a bridge which made a soft and
languid shape in the darkness, with spears of
light quivering down into the river. The Gare
d'Orsay looked like a wedding-cake on the quay
opposite. This station has stories and a basement,
and the Spanish train was leaving from the
basement. It was lying at the bottom of the
stairs, squat and green, and people were jamming
in a mass through the ticket-barrier at the last
moment. We were at the end of the line, almost
the last.

The ticket-collector was holding my ticket in
his hand. I looked down. The palm was deep,
thick and ridged, seamed with hard work and
long hours. He fingered the ticket for a time,
and bent over it looking at Barcelona while I
was guessing his eyes in the circle of darkness
between the rim of cap and the moustache.

"Is that where you're going?"

"Yes," I said.

He pushed the cap back off his forehead and
shook me suddenly by the hand.

"Comrade!" he said, still holding my hand tightly and looking at me, "good luck to you, comrade. And to all of them," he added. "I wish I was you."

The train had nearly gone. I jumped into the last carriage.

It was full. The lines of people's swaying bodies stood in the corridor, blocking out the profile of the town. The blue light was already turned on in most of the compartments, and people slept in mounds. At the same time I felt as if there was a trail of excitement, like gunpowder, running through from one carriage to another. How many of them are going there?

They had nearly all been sifted out before we reached the south of France. Three men suddenly got in at a small station, two of them very dark and sallow, with thin noses, and the other short and fair who seemed to be of a different race. One had his arm in a sling, and in several places the blood had pierced through the rough and dirty bandages. They talked a great deal together in Spanish, and seemed tired. After listening to them for a time we thought the young one might be Belgian.

"Are you going to Spain?"

They looked at me. One of them had big irises to his eyes, the brown fading to liquid yellow at the centre.

"Yes. Going to and coming from."

The Belgian spoke to me in French and said:

"We got cut off by the Fascist advance in the north-west. You know they're pressing on Irun. Their troops got between some of us and the coast. Some of us got through their ranks— it's like being hunted—and we took a ship and came to France. Now we're going back again by the other frontier."

I looked hard at them. They were the first militiamen I had seen.

They lay back and talked, their feet resting on the bench opposite. There were few people left in the train now. The militiamen wore canvas shoes with rope soles on their bare feet, and had on blue jeans. They rolled cigarettes fondly and dexterously and seemed now not tired at all, but excited and restless. They told a number of stories of Fascist atrocities which they themselves had witnessed. The Belgian said:

"I left my job and ran away to come and fight."

We roared suddenly into Perpignan, and a wild swirl of life charged up at the panting train, people hanging on the steps shouting and brandishing their arms and caps. Everybody seemed to know everybody. There was struggling in the corridor and faces pressed up swarthy and foreshortened against the windows from below. The train from Port Bou had come in from the other direction, too. People were festooned from train to train, going to and coming from Spain.

Since the beginning of the Spanish revolution, Perpignan has been like a kind of coaching-inn on the journey to Catalonia. One stops a few days going and coming, makes contacts, compares notes, settles plans for a fresh-hearted return to the attack. Perpignan has begun a new and fevered life, living on borrowed excitement at high speed. Everyone is there at some time or another. Secrets are whispered from mouth to mouth and from café to café.

When we stood in the station at Perpignan and the conductor blew his sharp bugle, the first smell of the revolution was in the air.

A tall youth with a languid neck rising out of his open, check shirt got into the carriage as the train moved off. He had on golfing trousers and carried a knapsack like ours. He looked round eagerly.

"Isn't it wonderful?" he said, at large. "Isn't it wonderful something like this happening while we're still alive—I mean, happening in the very middle of the kind of life we live. I work in an office. Now I'm off to see something real."

He was over-excited and strained, the colour showing in bright patches on his cheeks. The Basques looked with friendly curiosity at him out of their brown, closed faces. The Belgian boy said again:

"I left my work and ran away to come and fight."

"Did you?" The French boy began making

friends, and moved up closer. "I left my work, too. Threw it all up. Isn't it wonderful that something like this should really happen and give one a chance in life?"

He looked the typical office clerk, weak and too thin. He stooped a little from working in a cramped position on insufficient nourishment. Probably he really wore spectacles, but had taken them off to look dashing. He was gay and eager now.

The Belgian was hardened from having been at the front. Besides, he was a worker. He sat with his torn hands dangling from his knees, his deep young chest breathing in the close air of the carriage with difficulty. He had been so long fighting in the fields. His face was serene in its firmness.

"Well, we won't have anyone to envy when we're done."

"Why, anything can happen, absolutely anything," said the other earnestly. "What a life. A man just takes his gun, and off he goes, and begins making a new life."

"It's a bit hard at the front, of course," the Belgian said, to warn him a little, after scanning him. But he smiled very kindly.

"Oh, I don't mind. I'm ready for anything."

The day became hotter and stiller as we neared Cerbère. We got out because of the customs, and because there was a long wait. It was a hideous town. All the houses were covered with grey dust, and the empty bed of

a river lined with stones ran through the middle
of it, down which a grimed dog was snuffing
slowly, swinging his long tail. Nobody else was
about except a few children on the poor strip
of shingle facing the sea. They were pulling at
a net.

Everything seemed sticky and tired. A porter
on the platform, standing near the engine in
the pouring sunlight, was the only thing which
caught my eye with any pleasure, for he was
holding a gourd above his head and letting
water trickle down out of the spout into his
mouth. It was a long way from the spout to
the man's mouth, he had turned his head back
and up, and the water fell in a glistening
spray through the air. I felt cooled from
watching it. It would have been nice to be the
man.

The French customs were a formality. In the
range of mountains a tunnel had been bored
through into Spain. The train went through it,
really dived through the great mountain, and
emerged on the other side in Catalonia, where
everything was different at once.

We got out and walked about the casual
streets of Port Bou. The shadow of the plane
trees moved in the white dust. Cafés were
spread out under the trees, and here and there
militia-men sat with their backs to the trunks,
their 1914 rifles resting against their knees,
while they drank from long-stemmed bottles
or sat watching their cigarette smoke rise in

B

columns on the quiet air. At first it had been difficult to be allowed to leave the station and walk about the town. But we had the right papers to a revolutionary party on us and after a little shuffling they let us go, and I remember now the strong emotion of walking down between the files of these young Catalans in their blue militia overalls and shirtsleeves rolled up on the tawny arms, with their easy, friendly greetings. We saluted with the clenched fist as readily as shaking hands.

I was reluctant to leave Port Bou. I saw the revolution here for the first time, and the town was so lovely. The sea lay shining at the end of a lane between plane trees. At the party local, where we went, young and earnest commissars were seated round the room at tables in front of a backdrop of church banners like splendid tapestry. The whole room blazed with the gold striking up off the walls in the sunlight. Hoes, and some very old firearms, were piled in a corner.

"You see," one of these commissars in worker's overalls and open-necked blue shirt said to me, leaning over his desk: "People are so very anxious to help and do their bit that they bring everything they can find. This man brought his grandfather's pistol. On the 19th of July, many of us had only staves in our hands. But it didn't stop us winning, though now we do need arms badly. And munition. Especially, of course, munition."

When he said munition in that tone, I felt fully how anxious and eager he was.

There was no formality, nothing bureaucratic at all. We were all comrades at once and sat there talking familiarly between the burning gold of the hangings and the shadowless white walls. People came and went all the time easily. The day was soundless. The Catalan voices had a sour-sharp, rising inflection, jarring at first and then not jarring at all.

The train went out for Barcelona a few hours later. One day I shall choose to live in Port Bou.

Everything was changed in the train. The roaring was tremendous, people stampeding, singing songs. There were quantities of militia-men in all the compartments, their guns on their shoulders. In Catalonia a militia-man carrying a gun pays no fare for transport anywhere. At the end of one corridor two Civil Guards were standing apart, wrapped in their cloaks. The sinister shape of their hats blocked the windows.

"The Civil Guard is not really sure," a man sitting beside me said, pointing them out to me. "In all parts they have gone over to the strongest side. Of course they are with us here."

At least four guards looked at the tickets of the non-militia passengers and punched them in different places. We had lost sight of the Belgian and the earnest young Frenchman. Now I seemed to be the only non-Spaniard present. I felt quite pleased. People talked

Catalan on all sides, and it seemed to be full of Xes. I picked up a Catalan newspaper from the floor and began reading, picking out the words which were like Spanish and listening for their appearance in the conversation, and tried hard to construe.

The countryside was flying away from us on either hand and presently we came to Barcelona. We knew Barcelona because we had been there before in bourgeois days. Now we stood at the entrance to the station with our knapsacks on our backs and thought how overgrown with dust everything seemed to have become since then. A line of horses stood drooping their long thin necks in front of some cabs. There were no taxis, because these had been abolished. Still, people with luggage must be brought somehow from the station.

We walked through the rising dust as far as Columbus's statue. There was a group of cigarette sellers there now, their wide trays held in both hands and balanced from their necks on broad straps. Their money bags were pinned to their blouses under their chins with safety pins. We stood there with them, looking up the Ramblas, under the huge blue sky which seemed to droop and press down upon the charged atmosphere. Electric currents ran past us in the air. The crowd was moving in a compact mass up the Ramblas.

Columbus himself, perched high on the ornate column, had turned his back and was pointing towards the port. I looked. There were warships in the port. They were foreign and lay like a row of dozing sharks, showing their pointed noses to the town. For the first time I felt the civil war there, half a mile away.

II

ROUND THE TOWN

(*Narrative by Mary Low*)

WE DECIDED TO TAKE A STROLL ROUND THE CITY
and get a bird's-eye view of the changes.

The first feeling is one of liberation, as though
the city were emerging into fresh air and light.
I remembered the former feeling of religious
domination, with the church holding Barcelona
under the dark, sad shadow of its wing. Now
even among the alleys fanning out round the
cathedral there are no more sliding forms to
be seen, grazing the walls with the fluttering
black feathers of their robes. Two militia-men
sit on guard at the cathedral gate, their rifles
on their knees and the tassels swinging down
from their caps on to the bridge of their noses,
chasing the flies.

"Can we go in?" we asked. Behind the
backs of the seated guards we could see the dark
vaulting looping up in curves. We wanted to
see what changes had been made.

One of the guards looked languidly at the sun,
jutting down in a point between the roofs of
the dark alley. The other looked at us out of a

smooth face which seemed as though it had been carved from polished wood.

"There is no right of entry, comrades," he said.

He smiled, and his voice was friendly, but something of the dignity common to all Spaniards coloured his tone.

Footsteps moved in the building behind his back and the cavernous black recesses of the cathedral gave back the echo full-throatedly.

"We only wanted to see what they're doing with it."

"Well, it's to be put to a decent use at last. They're making an educational centre of it. But it isn't ready for showing yet."

We walked down the cobbles of the dark lane crouching against the flank of the buttresses and came out on to the front terrace. We were in the full sun here. The steps led down into the square below where children were playing. The beggars, who used to stand there whimpering in their regiments and showing a serried rank of sores for pennies have all gone. I only saw one beggar in Barcelona this time, apart from the gypsies. He was a very old man, drunk, who had only one leg, and used to hold open the door at one of the underground stations.

We began to walk about the narrow streets which wind in and out between the main thoroughfares. Every now and then a big sheet of white paper pasted over the name-plate of a shop or business made us stop and look. It said: "Taken over by . . . " and then followed the name of one of the workers' parties. The houses were hastily scrawled with big initials in red, the names of parties to which they now belonged. It was extraordinarily exciting. I looked about me. A feeling of new strength and activity seemed to radiate from the crowds of people in the streets.

We went back again into the Ramblas and stood looking up and down. Everything seemed to be centred here. Housefronts were alive with waving flags in a long avenue of dazzling red. Splashes of black or white cut through the colour from place to place. The air was filled with an intense din of loud-speakers and people were gathered in groups here and there under the trees, their faces raised towards the round disk from which the words were coming. We went from one group to the other and listened, too. It was nearly always people speaking of the revolution and the war, sometimes a woman's voice, but mostly men's. Between the pauses, snatches of the "Internationale" burst out over the crowd.

We walked about in a feeling of air and light. On a tree-trunk which we passed some flowers and ribbon had been nailed where a man fell fighting. Militia-men and sailors passed us in bands, with their arms linked, or else went roaring down the parallel roads in lorries with their guns held up above their heads, the sunlight darting off the barrels. The barracks had been torn down and a plain, full of white dust, lay open in their place.

There were crowds of little booths lined up under the trees on each side of the centre walk and as we went along I began to look at each in turn to see what everybody seemed to be selling and buying so busily. At first there were old women, sitting with their knees spread wide under the mass of skirt, trays of sweets on their knees. The sweets were green, amber, brown, and black, each in the little pile of its own colour, cut into squares and each square wrapped in glazed paper. They were transparent, like little bricks of coloured water piled up and shining in the sunlight. Next there were men squatting on the pavement in their white shoes, with rows of red silk ties and handkerchiefs embroidered with the sickle and hammer spread out before them. Afterwards, endless stalls of militia-caps stretching out tirelessly. Finally, there were the badges.

I went to one stall and examined them curiously. There were all kinds and shapes, made out in the initials of the various parties. Some were very attractive—big silver shields, with the sickle and hammer in red, or else in white on a background like a red star, and then squares divided diagonally into black and red, the Anarchist colours. It was astonishing how many different sorts there were, and how many people selling them. I looked round me on the Ramblas. Nearly everybody wore a badge of some kind pinned to his shirt. So a whole new little industry had had time to grow up already round the revolution.

Beyond the badge-sellers again were the tobacconists, with their trays full of coloured packets and cigars from the Canary Islands grouped in bunches. I ran up to one old man whose tray was almost empty, just as he was preparing to move off.

"A packet of 'Elegantes,' please."

"Impossible, I'm closed," he said severely, snapping down the lid of his tray as if it had been a shop blind.

A barrel-organ came down the street beside us, trundelled by two men in velvet trousers and torn shirts. Their bare forearms were tattoed with women with red pouting lips and opened fans. They stopped under the shade of a tree, and while one leaned at leisure against the trunk and turned the handle like a slow windmill, the other strolled round for the pence. We stopped to watch and listen. The organ was grinding out the "Internationale" in a lolling, hop-a-long way, with extra notes thrown in plentifully here and there. The big initials of the Anarchist trade unions were painted across it.

Quite suddenly the people in the street began to disappear. They seemed to be sifting out, draining away in all directions. The sun was blazing down now on the bare broad pavements, with only a few loiterers hanging about in the shadow of the houses. A clock struck one.

Breá spoke to a man who came out of a shop on the other side of the road to put up the shutters.

"Surely you don't still have the siesta here?"
He looked surprised.

"Why not?" he said.

"Do you mean to say that you shut up everything and go to sleep from one till four during the revolution and the civil war?"

He stared at us from large languid eyes as if the sun had struck us.

"People have to rest," he said. "It's like Sundays. We don't stop work on Sundays because of religion. We don't think about that any more. But people have to rest and amuse themselves, especially our heroic militias at the front."

"So they don't fight at the front on Sundays?"
He shrugged.

"It would be difficult to find the enemy. On Sundays, the Fascists have mass all day."

Life in the town seemed to have come to a dead end for the time being, so we thought we would buy the local papers and get an idea of the Press in some quiet spot. The cafés looked tired and empty, so we walked on looking for a park or a square with some shade. Passing down two or three cool, dark alleys between the leaning houses we came into a little square with a Christmas tree growing unobtrusively in the middle.

The square was backed by the wall of a church.

We walked round the building, looking up at it. The entrances had been blocked up with bricks, which showed a fresh red against the old stone face. A newspaper-seller was seated at the foot of one of these walls, his wares spread out on the ground round him, leaning back under the shadow of his cap-tassel. Above his head, two words had been chalked on the stone: "no passaran" (they shall not pass).

I bought two or three of the most representative papers, while a rose window without its panes gaped down at me like a great empty eye.

The air was by this time full of the most curious and inviting tastes. At the interstice of two narrow streets I saw a line of three chickens spitted on an iron stave and turning slowly over a fire. Hot grease ran over them and dripped methodically. Opposite, in the entrance to a bar, crowds of militia-men were standing with their elbows on a glass rail and dropping the curled bodies of long-nosed little fish off the end of tooth-picks into their mouths. Over the entrance to another food shop clusters of fruit were tied up in rich bundles and inside cheese and sausages dangled from the ceiling.

We ate some rice, full of little sea shells and red pepper. At other tables people were rollicking, and a sense of great well-being and friendliness filled the room. Good things abounded. There was strong and sweet wine in our glasses, and the prices were those which even we—for to-day, at least—could pay. Once or twice snatches of revolutionary songs blew in through the ever opening and closing doors.

Coming out, I saw that at least one thing had remained unchanged in Catalonia. The lottery, the eternal lottery, like a veil of illusion still preserved its glitter for Catalan eyes. On the corner of almost every turning a blind man or old woman sat on a folding stool, their white sticks at their sides, and sang in the same slow, unchanging voices:

"I still have two left, two equal parts left for the draw to-morrow."

Or it might be five, or three. The mournful cry pursued me from street to street. Sometimes the blind vendors walked, holding their tickets out in a fan before them. The even tapping of their white sticks against the pavement could be heard as a warning long before they arrived.

I decided to have a ride in the tram and survey the rest of the town whilst Breá went away to report our arrival to the Spanish Workers' Party.

The trams tread on each other's heels in the Ramblas like a string of yellow beans. One or two have open top stories, and I waited until one of these came by and then climbed on board. The trams are painted a smooth yellow colour, with the trade-union initials on all of them in red and black lettering. As I sat on the roof, with the broad leaves of the trees fanning my face as we sailed by, I waited with warm anticipation for the conductor to come and sell me a ticket, eager to pay for my first collectivised tram-ride.

He came presently, wearing a grey-green uniform with the cap pushed on to the back of his head. It was very hot.

"I would like to go to the end of the line," I said.

He looked doubtful.

"Are you sure you know where it goes to?"

"I haven't any idea," I said, "but I feel like going there all the same."

He laughed, and showed square white teeth in a dark-lipped mouth.

"All right, if you feel like going up the mountain, comrade."

"Where can I go from there?"

He began to be interested in my afternoon's programme, and suggested a few combinations, leaning easily with his arms folded on the back of the opposite seat. It was the slack hour and there were few people in the tram.

"After all, the best would be to take the aerial car down to the beach and then you could bathe."

I thought so too.

"How does it feel to work in a collectivised business?" I asked.

His eyes lit up with a curious flame.

"The revolution is splendid," he said. "We all work hard, but we work for ourselves, you see —no more bosses, but fair pay, and our committees run everything. It works much better than before. Of course all this belongs to us now," he said with a fine sweep of his hand showing the following string of trams. "You saw the trade-union initials on all of them? But that's nothing, you ought to see the new ones we're doing—all red and black, the union colours."

I felt that by rights they should belong to the community rather than the union, but he was splendidly enthusiastic.

The tram began to groan and pant and I found we were going up a steep incline between trees and imposing houses. Party flags fluttered from many of them, others remained dark and deserted with their white shutters folded over the windows. As we rose even higher we came to residential districts where the houses were set back in gardens full of violently coloured flowers, and the broad backs of palm leaves shone in the still and heavy air. Big red and white streamers were slung up between the trees, announcing a hospital for wounded militia-men, or a home for workers suffering from lung diseases. At the grilled gates the militias of the guard had set out their wicker chairs on the pavement and waited in the sun with a red flower in their mouths.

On a high hill, full of green lanes, where we finally came to a stop, I walked about for some time, enjoying the warm, fine air, and eventually found the little overhead car which swings down on a cable over the port to the seashore. It seemed a good thing to take the tram-conductor-comrade's advice.

The car was a square box, with windows, and a wheel on the roof under which passed the cable. I stood and looked out, while we swung into the empty blue bowl of the sky. Far, far below, like a painted landscape, lay the port and all the shipping and the houses crowding back into the town. Beyond the port a faint frill of surf was rising along the pebble-ridge, but within the harbour the water lay still and flat like a sheet of dark, transparent glass.

We landed on a steel tower and came down in a lift. I set out at once for the beach.

Going through the turnstile, the first thing to be seen were rows upon rows of cabins like the galleries in a bee-hive, and behind them a pink pile of desolate buildings which I supposed to have been once a casino, or something of that kind, but now dust-strewn. An elderly man with tattoed legs and blue trousers rolled up to the knees was walking about carrying pails of water.

"Where do I go?" I asked.

"Anywhere you like," he said, offering me the gallery with a handsome gesture.

"Is there anywhere where I can leave my knapsack safely—I mean, my purse and everything," I said.

"Anywhere you like," he said again. He gave me a candid look under a pair of white eyebrows like hedges and said with great dignity:

"People do not rob each other when they have all they need."

I felt he was right, and shut myself into a cabin without a lock, where I afterwards left all my things in perfect safety.

The beach was grey shingle, narrow and high, and the water up to one's neck almost on entering. There were numbers of people lying about there in the sun, or bobbing in the water holding a rope and swimming out to a buoy about a hundred yards away. Most of them wore faded cotton suits and were enjoying themselves thoroughly. I felt strong and contented, swimming out in the warm, very salt water and listening to the voices crying out distantly in Catalan from one group to another with the strange, rising inflection toned down by the soft air. Holding on to the rope, I began talking with a boy and girl with light hair and clear blue eyes.

"You're English?" they asked, with friendly curiosity. "People always say we're just like English people, because of being so fair."

"Do you think the revolution will come soon in England?" the young man asked me.

I was not very sanguine.

We got out of the water and the three of us lay on the beach and argued for a long time why Marx had not foreseen that the revolution would come first in places like Russia and Spain instead of in the highly industrialised countries. In the sun our fair skins burned.

c

I went back in the bus. It was getting late and the air was full of blue shadows. People were standing about under the arcades of the Plaza Macia, little spurts of red cigar fire leaping out on the encroaching dark. I sat down on a stone bench under the palms, and behind me the sound of falling fountains moistened the heat of the evening. Somewhere, down the aisle of the arches diminishing in the distance, two or three notes were plucked out of a guitar.

III

COMMUNAL LIFE

(*Narrative by Mary Low*)

THAT NIGHT WE ATE FOR THE FIRST TIME WITH THE militia-men and the revolutionary workers.

It was a vast room, filled with long, parallel tables. It was full already when I entered, and as I hesitated in the doorway, looking for a free chair, I saw rows upon rows of tasselled caps, and blue overalls everywhere. Lines of bare bronzed arms, with veins running out over them like loose string in the heat, rested on the white cloth. Two or three men, with butcher's aprons on, were carrying round bronze cauldrons, two to a cauldron, and ladling out the soup. The air was full of steam and voices.

"Here's a free place, comrade. Come on," a militia-man with a curled Assyrian beard called out to me, brandishing a spoon. A very old peasant, with a red Catalan bonnet on his round shaved head, moved up to make room for me.

I sat down. An avenue of faces stretched away on either hand. Noise and good humour. Opposite, the strict face of a young German was emphasised by three days' growth of stubble like straw, and a pair of oblong spectacles. Beside him was a man with long, soft hair, his wrists tapering out beyond the edge of his sleeves. He spoke to me in French:

"How long have you been here, comrade? I only came yesterday, because I couldn't find the fare to arrive any earlier. You see, I used to teach music at Lyon and it took me such a long time to earn the fare."

"I came to-day," I said. We smiled at each other. I thought he seemed glad to be sure of a proper meal.

The bearded militia-man was toasting us in light rosy wine which was being poured into our glasses from great squat bottles enclosed in wicker baskets.

"I just came back from the front," he explained. "My first leave. Of course it isn't so bad for you strangers when you go fighting, but I can't help remembering that they speak the same language as us and that some of them are workers, too. Whenever we can, we give them a call to come over and join us before we attack."

"Do they ever?"

"Oh yes. And most of the ones who don't are dirty Fascists, so it doesn't matter attacking them."

A short, broad woman in blue overalls and a red tie, with frizzy hair standing out round her head, leaned over and said to me eagerly:

"I was at the front, too. I got shot in the foot."

She had a very deep, husky voice and spoke softly, and it seemed as if the words were coming out from behind a velvet curtain.

"What did you do before you joined the militias?"

"I helped in my aunt's shop," she said, "but I like it better at the front, it's more exciting."

I asked the militia-man what he had been.

"A brick-layer," he said. His deep chest heaved with laughter suddenly under the Sam Brown strap. He pointed across at a brash-looking young man, his belt stuck with three daggers and a military whistle hanging from his pocket on a chain, and a pale, oval, thick-lipped face above it all. "Never guess what he was. We were at the front together and best friends before I ever knew it. Just imagine, an opera-singer."

He leaned over and punched his new friend in the chest, laughing so that his white teeth glittered in the midst of the shining beard.

"I was a hair-dresser," a tall young man a little way off leaned over to say. "And my friend here worked in a factory. We'll both be going off to the Aragon front to-morrow. I'm longing for it."

"They're all the same," the German said to me crossly, looking up and speaking for the first time. "All enthusiasm and no ideology. Of course I know they're very revolutionary, and so forth, but you have no idea how difficult it is trying to get them to put a little theory and order into things." He looked angrily over his spectacles, and then propped up Engels' *Origin of Family* between his plate and glass and began to read.

There was meat, but no knives. A militia-man with a red handkerchief tied over his head leaned across and offered me his stiletto, after having wiped it carefully against his sleeve.

I was at the local of the Spanish Workers' Party (POUM) where we were to live. Our stroll round the town had given us a glimpse of most of the various party locals and the life they lived. The great hotels had been taken over and put to this use as a rule, as well as many office buildings and banks. We had seen the massive pile where the Anarchists had installed their headquarters. It presented a high, con-cave face, with military rows of windows and had the trade unions initials posted up on it. Crowds were always grouped on its steps or streaming towards it down the breadth of the avenue. The parties affiliated to the Third International—about whose activities in the Spanish revolution the less said the better—occupied several handsome buildings. Later I visited some of them, and found the comradely atmosphere vitiated with starch and a kind of drill for marionettes imposed on the militants. Nevertheless, the hotel which they had taken on the Plaza de Catalunya was a fine place, banners on it and sand-bags in the windows, and a huge pair of portraits in charcoal hoisted up on to the front. These were naturally of Lenin and Stalin, never so inseparable as since the former's death.

Our place was more modest altogether, and pleasanter. I remember coming up to it on that first night. It had been the big commercial hotel of the town, in the middle of the Ramblas, and I had lived there at an earlier date. Now the sun blinds had been burned in the heat until the red stripes had faded and along the balconies a streamer curled a scarlet tongue. The entrance was chock-a-block with wine vats and baskets and chairs, and I remember being surprised at the casual disorder and good-humour which met me on the door-step.

There was a guard at the entrance, of course, as outside all party locals. They were six in number, and had pulled out wicker chairs into the cool shadow of the night, and sat there talking and singing in low voices. The gun barrels gleamed in the dark. A thin kitten played in and out between the rows of canvas shoes.

The night we arrived, a well-known French poet was standing guard, among the others. He was the last person I had expected to see.

"It's so extraordinary to be here," he said. "It's like living again." He put back his domed head and looked at the sky with its stars like large, white flowers.

I went into the hall. The lift was out of order and notices of the organisation were pinned on to the rungs of its gilt cage. In the bureau was sitting a strong, thin woman, with grey hair and a white apron. She had a revolver tied to her hip. At the other side of the hall glass doors opened on to the dining-room where I ate my first communal meal.

I went upstairs where a room had been assigned to me. The first floor had an open lounge, under a sun-roof, with chairs and tables at which people were grouped. Many sat on the banisters and on the broad shelf of wainscotting for lack of room. The room was badly lighted, detached faces and pieces of arms and legs swimming now and then into the pale glare where I could glimpse them. On a pile of trunks at the corner of the corridor, three girls in militia trousers were sitting, their knees clasped by their arms and red ribbons tied into their hair. I distinguished other faces. A tall man stiff as a pole, sitting absolutely still, his face hard and pale and the hair standing up above it. A Chinese face like a bowl. Another head, very fine and turned away like a startled hawk. Lips surmounted by an Adolph Hitler moustache in a round grey face. Then a clan of young boys sitting together under a lamp, their strong, intelligent gaze answering mine with friendliness.

My room was close to this lounge and looked out on to the Ramblas. I remember opening the windows and leaning over the balcony rails

to look on to the moving street. I felt deeply
moved. For the first time I had seen all conditions of people knit together in the common
delight of an idea, and the warmth of their
friendship touched me even while I stood alone
in my room. I was to be one of them.

I have a photograph which calls back the feeling
of the first days more quickly than my recollec-
tions, and shows some of us standing under the
sun-roof of a morning. It was the third day,
and I had got my militia uniform by then. The
tall German girl in her nurse's costume, its white
fading away into the white walls in the photo,
and her head overtopping the others in the
line, with straight hair and large, tender lips.
Then myself, standing with my hands behind
my back and the buckle on the new belt catching
the light. An Italian girl with spectacles, who
worked in the propaganda office, is beside me,
holding the hand of an older Austrian woman in
corduroy trousers. At our feet, the Belgian
miners with their fair, blown hair are sitting
with some boys from a factory in Marseilles.
We all look fresh and conscientious, under the
straight falling shafts of light from the glass roof,
but what makes the picture interesting is the
feeling of comradeship with everyone pressing
close together, touching each other and smiling.

This was part of the first foreign group in the
party. There were all kinds of us and we were
added to every day. The local was organised
so that most of the foreigners slept on the lower

floors and the Catalans at the top. I never understood this arrangement, which only served to cut us off from one another and prevented us from learning the language and understanding the Catalan habits of mind. Each floor had its guard. They sat there at night, relieving each other every four hours, half somnolent in the landing arm-chairs and pointing their guns down the well of the stairs.

I had only been there a few nights, when it was rumoured that the Civil Guard was about to rebel and march against us. Those were uncertain days, before the disbanding and reforming of the Civil Guard into two new and separate formations, mixed with surer elements. One was easily roused to anxiety. The organiser of the local, a silent, dark Catalan, his eyes pushed far back under the cliff of forehead, mobilised us all in preparation for the attack. We filed through the guard-room, shuffling one behind the other on our rope soles, and were handed out a Mauser and so many rounds of munitions apiece. I found the rifle an astonishing weight, and lugged it up the stairs with me in some dismay. All I had ever shot with was an air-gun, at fairs.

The mattresses were taken off the beds in every room, and we put them in the windows and then crouched down behind them with our guns. By balancing mine on the parapet which was thus made, I found I should be able to manage it without feeling the weight too much. It was hot and dark. A French Catalan girl, and a fat Dutchman and Breá and myself were kneeling in a row in my window.

For some time Breá was worried by the trucks and lorries which were lined up in the little square in front of the local. Seeing in the end that nothing was being done about them, he left his post and went looking for somebody responsible.

"Don't you think they could shunt all those cars out of the way? I mean, put them further off from the building or into the Ramblas?"

"What for?"

"Well, because if they attack from the front they can get behind those things and use them as a barricade. It'll be our loss. We ought to move them."

True Spanish nonchalance met him. The organiser waved a weary hand.

"Just suppose," he said, a faint anticipatory tiredness in his voice, "that we move them all and the Civil Guard don't come. Fancy having done all that for nothing."

Breá gave it up.

It was getting late and the tension was rising. Looking over the well of the stairs I saw Benjamin Peret, the French poet come sailing in as though nothing were afoot. He had been out all day and was quite uninformed. He looked at the range of stern faces with misgiving.

"Everything going on well?" he asked.

"Not very," I said drily. "We're only expecting an attack from the Civil Guard, and they might have caught you on the way."

He started, and gave a roar.

"The Civil Guard! Give me a gun. Where's a gun?"

There wasn't another gun. He snatched one hastily from a deaf comrade who was standing placidly by.

"He won't hear the shots, anyway," he said.

He joined us, and we stayed all night at the window. By degrees, a general feeling crept round that the Guard would not march after all.

"They won't come now," our Dutch friend said, composing himself carefully for a nap on the floor between two piles of overcoats.

"Why not?"

"Because it's past four-thirty."

"Do you think the Civil Guard is a train," Breá demanded, "that they have to arrive on time?"

Nevertheless the Dutchman slept and his methodical snoring kept us awake until daylight. The Guard did not come.

I had been in the local a week before I noticed that I had given up looking at myself in a mirror. One of the things which had always annoyed me about revolutionary women up till then was the lack of care they took over their appearance. Now I realised that one only bothers over feminine coquetry because of the shortage of larger interests allowed us in life under the capitalist régime. Nobody dressed up during the revolution in Spain. They forgot to think about it.

I saw the first contingent of men come back from the Aragon front. They arrived in the night. I heard the noise, and put on my overalls and came down. They were standing patiently in a serried mass under the lamplight, waiting to go in to eat, some standing on wounded legs or nursing smashed arms in stained bandages against their chests. Workers and intellectuals were mixed in the group, with here and there peasants standing together silently in the shadow of their wide straw hats. One or two had blankets flung across their shoulders or tied round their waists, but most of them had nothing. Material of every kind was so scarce at first. I went in and sat down with them while they had a late dinner. They were tired, some of them leaning down over their plates with their eyelids drooping, but full of good humour. I noticed, as always here in Spain since the revolution, the feeling of human sympathy that filled the room. The rough courtesy, too, a politeness born of the sense of equality.

We sat there chatting under the staring lamps, while other comrades in their white overalls brought round meat. A very young boy with a smooth olive face was sitting beside me. While everyone else was telling their exploits at the front, he remained silent, looking away. They brought his portion, and he took a dagger from his belt to cut it with. The meat was underdone, and the red juice gushed out.

The young boy pushed back his plate with a tired look.

"What's the matter?" I asked. "Aren't you hungry?"

"No," he said. "I don't want to see any more blood."

An older man, from the hill country, with his face showing like a brown wrinkled apple under the lamp, turned some oranges over in his hand.

"I rather would have had a sweet pudding," he said reflectively, with a reminiscent air. "In my village we all have a great tooth for a sweetmeat."

I looked at them sitting in rows down the long tables. When they told their war stories it was like no other race speaking. Their curious carelessness of death gave the tale a grand, exotic flavour. Yet something in that very flavour made it seem not so much carelessness of death as a deep desire for it—the desire for their foe's death and their own.

That same night, I stood with a group of captains who had come back, too. In the militias, the comrade in command wore no sign to distinguish him from his fellows and had no higher salary. Because of his greater ability he was obliged to shoulder a greater responsibility, that was all. The same comradely relations persisted.

These captains were from Murcia and the South, and one was an Italian.

"The Catalans are splendid fighters," they said to me, "but very poor soldiers. They don't run from the enemy, but it's impossible to keep them to their posts when it rains."

CHAPTER IV

A MEETING AT THE GRAND PRICE THEATRE

(*Narrative by Mary Low*)

A STRING OF CAVALRY BOYS, IN SHIRTS LIKE A fresh sky, formed a double barrage among the trees. Sitting there, well down into their saddles, with the leaves of the plane trees shining a lucid green above their caps, they whispered loudly to one another, and fidgeted. A whirl of flies was making a constant humming round the tired flanks of their horses, and round the big velvet nostrils which opened and shut in the heat like the gills of fish.

One of the riders, standing far off on the edge of the trees, raised his bugle and let two or three high notes drip slowly from its funnel.

The boys were all very young.

"Hardly any of the cavalry seem to be more than eighteen or twenty," someone said to me.

We elbowed slowly forward.

Over the heads of the crowd and the moving necks of the horses swinging impatiently, the Grand Price Theatre looked like a sugar house from a children's tale. It was shining white stucco, touched with red. From the outside it seemed small, with a narrow, uncompromising profile. Inside it opened up, and I stood, allowing myself to be pushed, on the threshold, looking into the deep cavern full of red light and the roar of voices.

A child stood on tip-toe to pin a P.O.U.M. badge on my militia-blouse. The blouse was stiff blue and crackly and resisted the pin. I helped to push it and jangled some money into the little tin box hung up round the collar on a thread of scarlet.

"Do you go to school?" I asked suddenly, thinking of the rush of new schools springing up everywhere. There had never been enough schools before. Behind us the roar of voices went on, magnified down a thousand tunnels of the air by microphones, swinging white discs from the corners of the hall.

"I do now."

She had an easy way of looking up at me, friendly and familiar.

"Since the revolution?"

"Yes. It's nice."

I had seen some of the schools, before and after, and ruminated on the change. It was different now from the old, droning monk-school, with the hundreds of inattentive children crammed into a single form, torn and super-annuated text-books one between five, and the same old humbug being taught day after day like a refrain. Or, worse still, what had been

D

the seminary for young ladies. The shell of one remained in a street through which I had recently passed, its notice-board still hanging by two nails from a ruined balcony. I remembered the dark apartment, full of pot-plants and massive furniture with gilt texts on the brackets, the oppression of tight corsets and three petticoats and of grilled windows. The education to resignation, the Spanish woman's load of Moorish heritage.

That was all changed for the child springing on her long, thin legs before me, and I thought of the high rooms with the light streaming into them, and of the youth and intelligence of the teachers and of the revolution. If we could push on past the rationalist education which the Anarchists were trying to impose, and go further and bring the children up according to Marxist precepts, then this revolution would never, never turn back.

I took the little seller, who spent her Sundays peddling badges for money for the wounded, and hand in hand we wedged our way over the shining, greased floor which creaked under the feet of the multitude. It had been fitted over the stalls of the theatre and now we all stood in line, pressing our chins over each other's shoulders, getting a sight of the room and the speakers.

The balconies were crammed full of people. Looking up, I saw tier after tier rising up and up, gradually reaching the dark shadows which filled the ceiling, so that the highest galleries of

all were scarcely visible. Red and white banners
were pinned along the railings, or hung down
towards us. There were slogans, and the names
of towns from which delegations had been sent.
"Without revolutionary theory, no revolutionary practice," was painted in huge letters above
a portrait of Lenin, which faced us from the side
of the stage. Trotsky was not there, but neither
was Stalin. There were white sickles and hammers everywhere. Over all the red light poured
down like continuous rain. Everything seemed
like the setting for a drama of monstrous propor-
tions, and my heart burned.

Faces became gradually visible. At the back
men from the militias were standing with their
chins up and their arms folded across their
breasts. Children wriggled in and out among
them. In the lower boxes, under the lee of the
balconies, the women were gathered together,
their hair glistening, while others, wearing
militia-caps on top of their curls, were sitting
more boldly on the steps among the men. From
some of the balconies, peasants with their
weather-beaten faces and sharp cheekbones,
were leaning out, grasping bunches of red and
emerald ribbons in their hands. Many of them
wore their hats, the colour of maze, the brim
rising upwards in a slow, serene sweep. They
listened so hard that their faces were as rigid as
masks.

It was a very responsive audience. The
moment any of the speakers touched on some

constructive measure to which the party was feeling its way, the listeners replied with cheers and loud, excited cries. There was hand clapping, and fists were raised. Anything really revolutionary which was said earned violent applause. But then it was a picked audience. The Anarchists, with their blunt-headed courage, were only there in small quantities, and the Socialists and official Communists were talking further down the street with their tongues in their cheek about the fight for the democratic republic. This Spanish Workers' Party was the only hope for the revolution, and it was a revolutionary party in spite of the mistakes it made and the opportunism it sometimes showed.

The whole scene in the Grand Price Theatre had been built up round the stage. The lighting and decorations were arranged so as to train the attention up towards the dais and concentrate it there in a torrent of colour and light. The table on the dais, the curtains, hangings, all within sight was red, with sickle and hammers in white, and the speakers themselves, under the arc-lamps, were a dark mass standing out stridently upon the bright field. Most of them wore the militia overalls. The Anti-Fascist Militias' Committee still existed, no one had even uneasily dreamed of its dissolution. We thought the Generality might have been dissolved, but the fault of that lay with the Anarchists who at the ripe time, when they held the strength in the street, had let the Generality go on through

scruple of libertarian non-governmental con-
science until it became a real force to be reckoned
with, and it was late to do anything.

Jordi Arquer was speaking when we came in.
Arquer was a centrist in the party which was
largely centrist. He was a little man, now back
from the front, and under a child's exterior hid
an astonishingly bad temper and a flow of words.
He had been at the Aragon front, and alone
wore the khaki which had just come in on the
battle-field, seeing that the lines of dark-blue
militia-men offered too clear a target to the
enemy from 'planes or in a sun-baked landscape. Arquer's mild blue eyes were fixed on us,
and out of the little puppet-face came the roar
that was filling the building.

He spoke readily of "rivers of blood," his
head back, and arms extended towards us. His
cap, pushed on to the back of his head, made an
odd square shadow on the red backdrop behind
him which moved about whenever he moved,
imitating his attitudes in a thick-fingered, clumsy
way. He was behind the table, which covered
him to the middle, and as the draping of the
table came down to the floor between us and
his legs, he rose up as from the middle of it
like someone sitting up gesticulating in bed. He
spoke in Catalan, and his voice rushed up in half-
arpeggios, the top note always broad and flat.

The others from the Executive Committee
sat together in a wedge on either side of him,
between the table and the walls. They blinked

in the white glare. I knew them all, and counted the ones who were there. Andres Nin, the best of all, the old revolutionary; and then the boy who was at the head of the youth section; next to him, Molins, in a light shirt under the militia overalls, and so looking more like one of the Three Little Pigs than ever—the most engaging of them, at any rate; Juan Andrade, his light, bold, haughty stare in a shark-like face, his huge height; Bonet, very tall too, with such a slow face—"The slowest face I ever saw," as a German comrade once said to me; Coll, later to be one of the heads of the police when the P.O.U.M. entered the Generality—and I can always hear him saying, in his blunt Catalan way, thrusting his head forward at the young woman who was asking for a passport so that her old father could leave the country, "and are you quite sure your father is not a Fascist?" Gironella, thin and effaced; there were others whom I forget. The versatile Gorkin, the party weathercock, was away talking elsewhere that day, and Rovira, with his Christ-like appearance, was still at the front. Later, a centrist of the party naïvely answered some criticism of the line of action by saying: "Why do we have to take Trotsky into account? After all, all he ever did in the Russian revolution was what Comrade Rovira is doing at the Aragon front now."

When the cheers following Arquer's speech had subsided, Nin rose to his feet. He is a

heavy man, short and thick. Now he wore a
blue militia tunic, and that and his curly hair
made him look young and eager as he leaned
with one fist thrust down on to the table and the
other hand held up.

At first the cheering poured over and over his
voice, drowning it, but when at last silence was
made for him his words came out deep and strong.
Nin speaks like a plain man. I haven't heard him
make embroidered phrases yet. He goes through
one thing after another point by point, and
hammers each of them into you, and the effect
comes from the simplicity and the sureness. He
is more effective to me than Gorkin, who has
spoken in Paris and was once banned from
speaking in London at a meeting organised by
the I.L.P. Gorkin spins out a lot which afterwards dissolves into smoke, though he is a born
orator.

The people react strongly to Nin. He has all
his past in Russia to back up his words and give
them body. All the same, a slight under-
current made itself felt when he got up to speak.
Some militia-men muttered and walked away.
Other people began whispering. Nin is the
revolutionary element, even though he has
considerably recanted during these last months,
and so those who are cooling off in a Liberal
direction go away. The vast majority who
remained, responded to him as a single man. I,
too, was moved, feeling the deep, excited breathing round me, and listening to the cries of delight

breaking out in the pauses, and seeing the man standing there, speaking with his face turned passionately towards us while the light beat down in torrents upon him; his gaze was so intent that he scarcely blinked.

It was over. While we were still shouting, and the men on the platform were still seated in a row and passing their hands over their wet foreheads, a band got gravely to its feet and broke into the "Internationale." We stood with our fists raised and sang and sang, the little light voices of the children cheeping in on the booming made by the men and mingling with the strange, raucous cry emitted by the women, who all have voices like peacocks. There was a feeling of tense emotion in the room. We fought to get out, and stood outside in the welter of the sunlight, talking about what we had heard, and patting the horses, and watching the people assembling with banners.

The procession began. In Barcelona, all the time I was there, there was always a procession on Sundays. The children went first, in little militia-caps striped with red, and carrying short square flags. Then came the band, busily playing the P.O.U.M. anthem, which was like a hurdy-gurdy tune, and a picket of cavalry behind them, the horses shifting uneasily sideways when they were made to walk so slowly, switching their tails over shining round flanks and pressing anxious noses into the hands and shoulders of the people who lined both sides of the street. Militias came afterwards, and more cavalry, and so on, until the Executive Committee appeared, strolling with their hands behind their backs or in both pockets, and chatting together under the shade of a huge flag.

Nin, off-stage, revealed himself sweet-tempered and rather owl-like as to appearance, wearing thick spectacles and walking along beside his fair Russian wife. People cheered as we went along, they climbed on to lamp-posts and waved their fists at us, and we raised ours too, in return. At the Plaza de Catalunya we had a long wait, as a procession of the F.A.I., and the P.S.U.C. (Moscowites) emerged from two different streets the same moment as we did, and there was some confusion in getting the huge, unwieldy crocodile under way. The Socialists marched much better than we did, their feet coming ringingly off the ground and every man the right distance from his neighbour; the Anarchists were much worse. This was before they had begun to bring out their famous posters saying, "Unite discipline to your will-power." I preferred our slap-dash way, we looked so friendly, and there was no stink of militarism for its own sake as there was later when I was leaving Catalonia. In those early days everything seemed to be on a rising tide. I was doing the Workers' Party's English publicity on a few pages mimeographed weekly, and thought I owned the world. Later, when I edited a printed newspaper in English, with other comrades helping, and sold 4,000 copies weekly and brought in money, and things seemed to be so flourishing, we were really on the downwards trend, because so much opportunism had already led to counter-revolutionary actions.

But that day at the meeting those first times were really in full flower, and we marched and raised our fists and felt air-bubbles in our shoes. The red banner brushed the trees all down the Ramblas, and on we went, the F.A.I. ahead of us, with their black flag flapping like crows' wings, singing "Sons of the People" for all they were worth. The Socialists were tagging along at the back. The air was thick with heat and dust. I can remember the hot smell of tar coming up off the road. We marched right down to the bottom of the Ramblas, because at that time we had not taken over the splendid building of the Bank of Catalonia and knocked out the counters to make a pillared hall, but had only a few rooms full of tables on top of a theatre.

I didn't mind the long walk since I felt full of enthusiasm. It was only afterwards, when we went to meetings every Sunday and marched home like this all the way, that the road began to seem long.

CHAPTER V

A FULL DAY

(Narrative by Mary Low)

THIS IS THE WAY WE LIVED AS A RULE.

The mornings were crisp and fine, with the cold of the night air still settled on the tiled flooring of the rooms. In the kitchen, cups of coffee were served, and fish or sausage sandwiches at the militia bar opposite the local. The kitchen was like the inside of a ship, wood everywhere, and portholes through which the cups were handed out. We used to line up there, in the wing of the dark woodwork, and stand one behind the other shuffling our feet and pushing each other's elbows, while the smell of wine being poured out from casks soaked the air. The men in the kitchen, on the other side of the porthole were all in white, and lifted the coffee-pots —which had long brass bases—out of the stove. When there were not too many of us we could come into the kitchen too, and stand leaning our elbows on the dresser, and stirring coffee, and teasing a fat, short white dog with a black ear, or the cat.

We went to the militia bar, too. It was in the

foyer of an old theatre. There was always a lot of joking at the counter. We read our papers there, craning over each other's shoulders. Afterwards, we began working.

At first we worked in the local itself: on the landing, or in the saloon where the militias sat, or else in our rooms, or in the rooms above the theatre opposite, where the Executive Committee lived. We used to sit at any free table we could find, our elbows touching, writing and translating with one hand on the dictionary. The men waiting a day, two days, to be drafted to barracks or the front swarmed round us, talking, carting tin helmets and making the butt of rifles ring on the paved floor, or sat along the wainscoting in rows like birds on telegraph wires. The talk was always political talk. Cigarettes were given out from an organisational office every day, and beds allotted, and people came in and out of the office all day long, although a hand-written notice pinned to the door pleaded, "Please do not disturb unless on urgent matters."

Everyone disturbed. We sat in the office armchairs, talking above the clicking of the typewriters and planting red or white flags into position on a map of Spain which was gummed to one of the walls. Papers were piled up everywhere.

There was no sense of discipline, but great friendliness, and a desire to collaborate. I was amazed at first at the lack of personal criticism,

of personalities of any kind. Though even that
crept in later, among so many other regrettable
things. Once, during the first days, before I
had got out of bad habits, I said, standing leaning
on the rail of one of the galleries which overhung
the central lounge:

"I don't like H—— much, do you? There's
something disagreeable about him."

I was met by a candid, anxious stare.

"Really? Did he say anything tendentious?
I thought his position was absolutely sure?"

I felt foolish.

"I don't mean that. I only meant I find him
rather bad-tempered."

"Oh."

Complete cessation of interest in the eyes, and
my interlocutor turned away to something of
more importance.

I learned not to do it. Afterwards, I didn't
feel that way anymore. It all faded in so much
friendliness, and we talked only politics and
felt sure of the revolution. Those were early
times.

On the other side of the square, above the
theatre, there was always a crowd of people on
the three flights of stairs. We had to go up and
down about two or three times a day, to fetch
documents or ask questions. People poured up
and down all day long, giving in their names for
adherence, coming to ask after their sons at the
front, coming to touch militia pay, coming for
information. There was no sort of control.

Anyone came in, and strolled about the room, while two or three comrades sat behind type-writers here and there and took down names and paid out money. People crowded in the windows and leaned for hours on the sills, looking up and down the Ramblas in the sun. A general atmosphere of good cheer reigned. Two or three militia-men sat in arm-chairs near the door, playing with the children or swinging their white canvas shoes. The absence of bureaucracy was enchanting.

Up three steps behind the big room, seething like a railway station, and behind a glass door was the small den into which the Executive Committee could just manage to squeeze them-selves. There was nothing of a holy of holies about this room, and nobody was awed by the idea of going to talk to the committee. People knocked and went in whenever they felt like it. When there were more people than the members of the committee inside, everybody had to stand up and leave the door open for the over-flow.

Afterwards, they put someone on duty outside the door, to find out why people wanted to come in, and sift some of them. I came up one day and found a peasant waiting to get in. He was standing there obstinately in front of the guard, his feet in flat Catalan sandals with blue ribbons winding round the leg and ankle, and a broad hat held in both hands.

"The comrades of the Executive say you have

to wait a moment. They're busy," the guard
was repeating.

"I don't want to wait," the Catalan said
placidly, turning his hat in his hands. "I'm
busy, too. I'll go in now."

"But you can't go in now. You must wait a
minute."

"Why should I wait for them?" he asked, not
impatiently, but serenely proud. He was broad-
shouldered and upright.

"Are we not all equal?" he said.

They let him in.

Often things happened like that at first, but
less afterwards. The party became more and
more bureaucratic as time went on, and soon,
what with the official participation in the government and the arrival of minor personalities from
much more tepid parties in other countries, a
way was opened to formalities and all kinds of
red tape. The net of bureaucracy began spread-
ing everywhere. The people were prevented
henceforth from showing that fine sense of their
worth and dignity, as the peasant comrade had
shown it, though of course the committee still
remained " *tu* " to all comers—even ministerially.

Lunch arrived at two o'clock, often rushed up
on trays to the crowded inner room where the
session continued unbroken over the plates of
food. At the local we worked on a boring system
of meal tickets. Someone was charged with
giving these out every noon to all demanders and
you were not supposed to be served with food

unless you could show one.   Whenever the tickets were given to one of our Catalan comrades to distribute, they were almost always lost or too few, or else the comrade went away somewhere else and forgot to give them out.   I have annoying memories of long waits in front of the firmly closed dining-room doors, when time was precious and appetites sharp.   One is not born Catalan with impunity.

Anyone could eat in Barcelona.   You only had to go to a local and ask for a ticket and it was given to you.   There was nothing of charity about it, just the normal rights of everybody all free and equal.   At every meal we sat down hundreds strong, with all kinds of people who were not party members and of whom we often knew nothing.   The food was plentiful but nearly always began with beans.   The Germans hated beans.   But they were always much too hungry to go without them.

One day the first provision ship arrived. Everyone was excited, and we all wondered what it would bring.   That ship promptly landed five thousand kilos of beans on the quay.

When we heard this good news, a wan look overspread the German faces.   They afterwards decided to form an Anti-Bean League.

At four in the afternoon we charged with our pencils again and the revolution seemed to be advancing in bounds on the backs of the type-writing machines.   We made our first broadcast one day, over a tentative post an electrician comrade had set up in a small cottage. That was a great day. Later, when we began to take over many buildings, and participated in the Generality, and had expanded so much, we had broadcasting stations everywhere, and gave big daily broadcasts, and it all became part of the routine. It was the beginning that was the excitement.

When we stopped for a rest and had any money in our pockets we went to the cafés. Café life is as flourishing in Barcelona as ever, only now one sometimes sees women there, too, instead of the eternal male heads clustered together over manzanilla. The cafés are collectivised. Over the bars, proud notices are hung up: "No tips accepted here." This is true. Seeing a waiter brushing eagerly over a shining counter with his broom, or hurrying towards you with a tray above his head like a ship under full sail, one notices with ease and delight that the old pence-crawling and servility is dead for ever, and instead a man is going about his work, himself master of all he surveys were it not that mastery like ownership has faded away into disuse in this new world and the words have lost their sense and vigour.

The waiter asks:

"What will you have?"

He bends over you.

You look up.

He is a young man, a young man like yourself, speaking to you with the perfect natural

E

politeness and gravity of a human being, and you remember that he has no boss now, that he probably sits on the committee every night, and that this café is clean and beautiful because he wants it to be. He is working now, as you might be tapping a typewriter.

"A coffee, please, comrade."

You both smile.

Afterwards, sitting sipping out of a glass and probably noticing that your feet are dusty, you decide to have a shoe-shine, if you are not wearing canvas slippers. The shoe-shiners generally wear black corduroy, and you see them haunting the corners of streets and the entrances to cafés with their shoe-rests hitched under their arms. We used to sit chatting to the shoe-shiners, who are mostly Anarchists, while they squatted at our feet moving their black, deft fingers round our shoes or pulling a taut rag over the toe-caps with balanced, sawing gestures.

The first time my shoes had been shined, I offered a tip.

The shiner returned it to me with a flourish.

"I have my union," he said, with great dignity. "I do not need your charity."

"I'm sorry, comrade," I said. I felt prickly with shame. "It's an old capitalist habit."

We shook hands.

There are numerous cafés, and we visited one after the other.

As you go up the Ramblas to the Plaza de Catalunya, there is first the Grand Oriente, with its brown front and gold lettering like a slab of gala chocolate and inside, bars piled up with round sandwiches—sweet pepper, garlic sausage, crackling of pork, fresh fish, little octopus, liver paste, ham-and-roquefort, and salt bacon. On another counter are thick-set doughnuts full of yellow jam, plum-cake, crystallised fruits, cream horns, nut-biscuits and marzipan patties. At the back of the room a few stairs lead down into a dining-room with an open hearth and massive mantel, and beyond that to endless billiard rooms where the low-hanging lamps in green shades, and the perpetual curtain of smoke make an aquarium-like atmosphere. At night the bar was crowded with people standing close together, as if they were travelling on the underground, laughing and drinking each other's healths, and militiamen on leave, bearded and in khaki, sitting untidily under an oriental canopy and singing songs.

Next came the Automatic Café, mechanised downstairs, and looking like a club lounge upstairs with tempered lights and tables set back in recesses. Here we ate steak sandwiches, and sat under the brim of the lamp while in the recesses up and down the aisle people with secrets whispered together. The patrols made their slow rounds at night from bar to bar, asking to see one's papers, and closing down the cafés at the official time. Besides them, often a bearded militia-man rose from a group round a table, and coming over to us saluted with his clenched fist and said:

"I ask your pardon, comrade, but would you mind showing me your papers?"

The courtesy was grave, a hint of cloak and sword about the Spanish gesture.

I took out my papers.

"By all means, comrade."

He bowed again and shook hands, his dark eyes kindling.

"Diaz, of the F.A.I. You excuse this boring formality, of course, comrade? One has to take so many precautions, these days, there are so many spies attached to the foreign Legations. You remember all those Nazi-looking types who used to live under the protection of the German Embassy? We're getting most of them put out of the country by this time, but it has made us perhaps a little too careful over all foreigners."

"Please sit and have a drink," I said.

He did and we talked.

Relations between the Catalans and the foreign comrades were becoming a little strained about that time, through no fault of the Catalans. They are a rough and ready race, and strangers coming to fight at their side had showed themselves too fastidious and exacting, instead of trying to understand and make allowances. They were inclined unwisely to stress their intellectualism, and to show off a boasted education. The Catalans, whom the long struggle for

freedom from the hampering backwardness of
the rest of Spain has rendered apt to fall back
on to nationalism, given the excuse, reacted
with wounded dignity mixed with a peck of
chauvinism. The word "foreigner" became
abusive. So afterwards, all rancour swept away,
they re-baptised us "internationals," which, on
the contrary, was a word of high and revolutionary esteem. The "internationals," with their
criticism, were inclined to forget that the com-
parison was too easy—a band of picked men,
selected from the whole world, to whom it
had been worth the struggle and sacrifice to
leave everything and come to Catalonia, as
against the average rank and file of a country
where culture is far from general.

There are other cafés which, at night, are
full of life:—the Euskadi, with its dark mirrored
woodwork, and Caneletas, where they grill
sandwiches for you over the fire and spread
them, still smoking, with cold mayonnaise, and
the American Bar with the dark, quiet room
stretching away into the shadows, and the
Café de las Ramblas, old-fashioned and uncomfortable, with hard chairs and marble-
topped tables. Here the young schoolmasters
of the revolution were usually gathered, their
eager faces studying plans for schools and
educational schemes which they spread out
over the tables, or making up the format
of scholastic reviews. At other tables, the
representatives of the English Press, a poor,

grey-looking group, sipped cocktails and failed to make contact with the highly-charged atmosphere. Sometimes I sat down at their table for a short while and talked to them. They understood nothing of what was really going on, and cared less.

They talked mostly personalities. I came away tired with the stings of their little individual hates. I had the impression of a closed citadel, impenetrable to new life.

At other tables, people would come in, flushed and loud-voiced, from a meeting somewhere. The party orators were always there for a moment or two, coming back in a car with a streaming red flag on the bonnet from a town in the north or a village where the peasants had stampeded and shouted themselves hoarse with excitement. I remember Pilar Santiago, coming back after speaking at Port Bou and falling down in a heap on one of the horse-hair sofas. Everyone was tired out and happy. She had on striped stockings, and flat shoes like boats, and a sleeveless dress, and looked so beautiful, with her head like a violent-lipped angel.

"It was a wonderful meeting," she exclaimed, clasping her hands together, and leaning towards me over the table. "The people were so splendid and cheered so much. They felt it all. I was telling them about the front, and Irun, and how we *must* triumph over Fascism, not only for ourselves but to stop the exploitation for our children who are little now, but who one day—Oh," she said, "the revolution *must* triumph."

The colour rose beneath the white skin of her cheeks. It made her eyes look blacker.

"Do you like speaking?" I asked. "Do you prepare everything very carefully beforehand?"

"No," Pilar Santiago said earnestly, shaking her head. "I begin to talk to them, and then I feel it all, you know. It's wonderful, I see everything I say coming true. But sometimes there are terrible moments, like to-day, when I was speaking about our children and the Fascists, and I could not stop the tears from running and running down my face."

She is very young, torn between tenderness and flame.

There is one more café where we often went, and that is the Moka. The Moka had a bad reputation—possibly because it was very luxurious—and was supposedly full of disguised Fascists. Nevertheless, it was noticeable that the militia-men back from the front always spent their first morning or afternoon's leave seated on the broad terrace in the sun and watching the life of the Ramblas, which reached its most lively and vivid at this point.

Inside, there was certainly something unprepossessing about the clients. They were too smooth, and had rings on fat white hands. But the café was an oasis of comfort, with each couch set back in its own recess and topped by a little thatched roof all to itself, very low armchairs full of cushions, and a tempered light. A delightful smell of fresh-ground coffee floated in the air. In another room at the back there were little gilt chairs round marble tables, and exotic birds flying about in an aviary which occupied the whole of one of the walls.

When we left our last café, it was always to return to work again. Later, our nights ended inevitably at the press, but in these early days we had no other offices but our bedrooms, and there we sat until the small hours, slamming at typewriters in the unshaded glare of an electric bulb, while the street roared by below the window and finally ebbed and eddied into silence.

VI

THE ARAGON FRONT

(*Narrative by Juan Breá*)

FOR DAYS WE HAD BEEN WAITING AT THE BARRACKS for the order to march. There was a scarcity of arms. The F.A.I. had what was ⸱left—old Mausers dating from the beginning of the Great War, and ammunition—and showed a natural reluctance to part with them. Day after day we assembled in the courtyard and stood about for hours in the burning sun. Towards evening we were dismissed home to our quarters, and it was for to-morrow.

Other parties were in the same plight. Even the F.A.I. could not send out enough of their own troops.

Our group made up the International Lenin Column. About fourteen different countries were represented in the Column under the command of Russo, an Italian who had served as an officer with the Italian army in pre-Mussolini days. Russo was tall and swarthy and came from Naples. He had slightly dead, bloodshot eyes, always half closed, and used to remark readily:

"They all like me. They say I'm sympathetic and take me into their confidence. 'Come on, Russo,' they say, 'you're our friend.'"

Afterwards, in the yard, he tried to get us into order, remarking wearily:

"Can't you stand in line? You *must* stand in line, damn it."

He didn't care about discipline, but he was a good military expert.

Second in command was Calero, a barrister from Murcia. His red hair was thinning now on top but his eyes were bright and shining, rolling like blue marbles on fire in the darkness when, with the lights turned down over a rum punch, we sat round listening to poems. His beautiful voice vibrated then like a stringed instrument. Apart from that he was always laughing, slapped us readily on the shoulders and called us "his lions."

Calero lived at home, and only came daily to the local, but Russo lived in like the rest of us and was supposed to be quartered in barracks. As barracks offered a very rough and ready accommodation and were some way out of town, he spent most of the nights he could in the first-floor lounge at the local. Passing through in the red glare of a lantern, when we came back home from the cafés, we could see him hunched up in a pair of plush armchairs in his blue jeans, with somebody's kidnapped pillow thrust behind his head.

During the daytime, while we were still

waiting for orders, we all went together to the
barracks and ate meals with the veteran militia-
men. We ate sitting in opposite rows on wooden
benches, and had tin plates, and cups the size
of little soup tureens. One cup did for every five
men. The food was better than at the local, but
we had to serve ourselves. The afternoons were
long, with nowhere to sit in the courtyard except
the hot stones, and political quarrels were always
breaking out among the groups of men who
squatted under the arches.

We took photographs, some of us sitting about
on the ground and the others standing behind,
with our regimental flag flying over our heads,
and grasping *L'Action Socialiste* and *La Lutte
Ouvrière* well in evidence in our hands. We had
been given khaki clothes by this time, and red
flannel neckerchiefs, and light shiny belts with
little boxes on them for our ammunition. Later
came the tin hats, and on the last day, arms at
last.

When they began to be handed out to us, and
we knew we were going to the front at last, we
climbed aboard some old Ford lorries that were
standing in the yard and stood up with our guns
in our hands and cheered and cheered.

That was at four o'clock in the afternoon.
It was nine at night before we got going. By
that time we were tired, and our first enthusiasm
had worn away. The miles to the station were
heavy going, though the people cheered. We
had packs on our backs, with straps that cut

into the shoulders, and as we marched down the Ramblas in the half dark quickly gathering, the women who lined the way thrust flowers into the barrels of our rifles. We moved between a hedge of clenched fists, our own tired fists raised intermittently. People sang the "Internationale" and great flares of red, like spears of blood, smeared the sky, and the windows in the Via Layetana seemed all on fire. The night drew down as we neared the station. The shoes of the horses in the cavalry detachment struck sparks off the road.

As we climbed into the train, people swarmed into the station after us, on to the narrow platform, and stood there shaking our hands and laughing and shouting to us as we leaned out of the windows. A little boy got aboard somehow, and hid among the packs in the corridor. When Russo found him, and put him out, he stood still and sad on the edge of the platform, letting himself be pushed by the crowd and only repeating over and over again: "I want to go to the Aragon front."

We were going to Huesca, though we looked as if we were going to a fair. We were going to the front, and would reach it quicker than we thought. Barcelona offered us its homage as if we were a whole army arriving in triumph but really we were only a single column, the third column of the P.O.U.M., going out to victory. We had no doubt of this, for the revolution is no game of dice in which either the ace

or the six may impartially turn up. We were
sure we were going to win, and woe to him who
doubted.

The train was as long as a minister's title.
The people seeing us off were in shirt sleeves
and raised cries of "Long live the world revolution." Romantic bourgeois legends about sad
good-byes all come to an end here. Ours was
completely lacking in romantic melancholy. We
had no time to be sad. Who would have thought
of being sad, in any case, while people looked
at you with such envy that their eyes might have
snatched your rifles from your hands, people
who will be coming to join you to-morrow?

Sabadell, Lerida, Barbastro, and other villages,
received us triumphantly. Lovely girls came
to the train carrying flowers in one hand and
a ham in the other, and gave them to us with
their most revolutionary smiles. Our journey
seemed like a ride in a tram, the enthusiasm
of the people made it seem so short.

From Sariñena to Sariñena there is a distance
of five miles—that is to say from the railway
station to the town. Here we left the train in
the morning, only to take it again in the
afternoon. Was it a counter-order or war
tactics? Only the command knew, and we did
not find out.

A return to the train once more; but now
we found that our train, which had lost nothing
in size, had been bereft of the splendour of first,
second, and third class. We were in a cattle

train, and the atmosphere let us know it. We sang to cheer ourselves. Everyone had to take his turn at singing, and the defaulter suffered a forfeit voted by the majority. This was generally to fetch water at the next stop, or to walk on all fours, or else to recite a prayer, and the latter seemed a large punishment for so small a sin as having failed to sing a song, apart from the fact that many had sincerely forgotten all their prayers. Did we, I thought, seem anything at all like the vandal red Marxist hordes about whom Franco talks on Radio Seville? We were more like children.

We reached Barbastro. Eat and sleep as quickly as possible, was the order given out that night. We accomplished it. We slept in an empty convent, lying in rows on the floor of a dormitory on mattresses.

A noise woke me suddenly only an hour later. A light moved near the door, whispers, and something glinted on a blade. There were uniformed figures in the doorway. A night raid.

I jumped to my feet.

"Fascists! The house is full of armed Fascists!"

An indescribable scene of confusion and excitement followed. This was succeeded by hilarity or groans of bad temper at having been wakened when we discovered that the intruders were part of our cavalry who had come out by another way.

At three o'clock in the morning the bugle woke us again. We formed up.

"I'd only just dropped off."

"I'd scarcely been to sleep at all."

"Where are they taking us now?"

Somebody answered:

"We're going to Alcala del Obispo."

The front, the real front at last.

Alcala del Obispo is a little village of the kind which abound in Spain to-day: a tower which was once a church, and the ruins of some farms.

It was seven o'clock in the morning, and there were more than five hundred of us, but I have yet to see a village with so many hotels. From every house there came:

"Come in here, comrade, we've an extra bed in here. Come in, anyway, and we'll fix you up somehow."

Half an hour later, the entire company was settled in and sat down before the sweet-smelling cups of coffee which awaited us. And after that, rest.

I still remember that knowing smile which greeted my remark that if I slept now I shouldn't be able to sleep at night.

"You know, at the war you must sleep when you can."

We used the wooden painted statues of the saints to light the fires for cooking our meals. They had been thrown out into the square when the church was burnt. Now there was a shortage of wood, so one day we chopped up St. Eduvige, virgin and martyr, and the next day Anthony of Padua, and even St. Apapucio, until it came to the turn of the patron saint and bishop of the village.

The peasant women stood on their doorsteps, watching. One of them seemed rather troubled.

"Well, comrade," I called after her, "it weighs a bit heavy on your heart to see him broken up, after all, I suppose?"

She gave me a vague, moist stare, crowded with two or three centuries of ignorance.

A man standing near replied for her.

"Weighs a bit heavy on her heart, does it? Well, if she knew the weight of that lump of wood and had been forced to carry it round the town on church festival days every time there was a procession. . . ."

"At least they paid you something for doing it, didn't they?"

"Pay? Not a bit of it. The priest used to say it was an honour."

"And supposing you refused the honour?"

"Well, I tried to once, but as I was working on his farm I had to go for six months without finding a job."

I said to another woman, who was leaning against a lintel with her arms folded over her heavy breasts:

"What about you, comrade? Did you have to cart the bishop too?"

She replied:

"I've only got one thing to say, and that's that ever since the wooden statues went out of the church the food has been coming into the village. My man and my sons have got work now. We don't have to go short any more. I don't mind whether you say you're red or blue, we don't know about politics, it's not our business. But I do know that those wooden saints have been good for something at last. Because, you know," she added, "though we sometimes had enough wood before there was often nothing to cook with it."

Everything is run according to bugle blasts, and I begin slowly to get used to this new language. When, in the middle of the day, the bugle sounds, I have not much difficulty in knowing that it is for lunch. But when we had a second bugle blast right in the middle of the meal, I failed to understand at all.

"What's that for?"

"Form up."

A torrent of protest.

"But whatever for? Where are we going?"

But the captain only replied:

"You must form up, damn it."

"Listen, comrade," said a truculent militia boy with a shadow of stubble beard. "I'm not a parcel to be sent without knowing where I'm going, and without even having finished my meal."

Russo considered him out of his dark, sleepy eye.

"Well, I haven't begun mine yet, but I'm forming up."

"But why, Russo?"

"Because we're going into the firing-line."

F

And the incident was closed. The young man took his place in the line, only murmuring: "Well, that was all I wanted to know."

Many others, besides ourselves, were novices. I think that they and I will not easily forget that first moment when we climbed into the lorries which were to take us over the four miles which lay between us and the firing-line.

It was one o'clock of the afternoon, and hot. We followed the main road, and then turned off into a smaller road. We were leaving the flat, Aragonese plain and the ground began to undulate, running towards some foothills, and beyond them, mountains. The road was white, dust rose heavily round the wheels of the lorries. On either hand, the landscape stretched away, savage and sterile, covered with thorns and thistles. From time to time, a bouquet of trees bordered the road. Sometimes there was a house, or a man ploughing. He moved very slowly behind a team of oxen, and had a coloured handkerchief knotted over his head, with fronds of cool leaves fastened into it and descending to cover his cheeks against the sun. At the corner of a field, the inevitable dog awaited the return of the plough, a pool of saliva gathering below his hanging tongue.

As we went on, we could hear the stamp of the cannon growing louder with every minute, and the clicking of the machine-guns. Every time the ground rose up a little, Huesca appeared suddenly within sight, a city drawn in white chalk, and we seemed to be looking at it near and clear as though through a spy-glass. The next moment the ground would dip again, and so we continued to lose and find Huesca in this way on our horizon. It was seated on a slight hill.

On the way other lorries passed us. When we saw them coming, in a veil of dust, full of soiled militia-men, we raised our fists and shouted out to them:

"À Huesca! À Huesca!"

They shouted back, and passed us in a roar.

We saluted the peasants, too, whom we saw from time to time standing on the edge of the fields. They looked at us with their deep, placid stare, standing immobile, and then remembered suddenly and raised a hasty fist like a stage monkey who has almost forgotten his part.

The cannon were snorting. The noise raised exclamations of enthusiasm in our lorry.

"That's ours at work," the chauffeur told us, with the air of an old customer.

We sang a bit and laughed too much, as always when one is a little afraid. Some of us, who had never had a gun in our hands before, were learning hastily how to load and unload and take aim while the vehicle jolted on.

In a moment we turned a bend in the road and saw that the lorries ahead of us had already drawn up. The men were getting down from them. It is really the front, now. The sudden stop, which threw us on to each other, served to hide our emotion.

Eleven lorries were lined up along the edge of the road. They had taken advantage of a group of trees in order to remain hidden from the Fascist aeroplanes. We formed up in fours. The day, with a high blue sky, seemed like a bowl of silence, pierced now and then by a shot from the cannon. The machine-guns, making a noise like typewriters, continued champing, but seemed like a noise outside the bowl, they were so little able to impose themselves in the absolute quiet of the day. Over there, the black wings of one or two Fascist aeroplanes were drawing arcs on the edge of the sky.

A wire fence, dividing off the fields, and the mountain slope before us, are all that remain to divide us from the firing-line. But now we learn that we are not to climb that slope until to-morrow. We are emergency forces, waiting in the rear.

We all piled through the wires in the fence, and began looking for a place protected by trees in which to camp. We threw ourselves down on the ground here and there in the shade, with nothing to do until new orders should come through. It was hot and dry. Some men went for water, and now that the first emotion had been appeased we began to think about our interrupted meal and to tighten our belts. Calero, coming round and slapping us all on the shoulders, told us we would eat the meal of our lives in Huesca to-morrow.

VII

THE FIRING LINE

(*Narrative by Juan Bred*)

THE IDEA OF WAITING ABOUT INACTIVE FOR
another twelve hours, with the firing-line only
just out of sight, made us impatient, and we
went to find our lieutenant. He was standing
a little way off, surveying a group who were
being given a tardy lesson in the manipulation
of fire-arms, and told me that the big attack
on Huesca was probably due tomorrow.

"We very badly want to have a glimpse of the
firing-line without having to wait till to-morrow,"
I said. "We want to know what it's like."

"Do you mean it?"

"Yes, of course I do. What's the use of
waiting around here?"

"All right. Fetch your guns and we'll pay a
visit to the machine-gun section."

He was rather pleased at being able to give
us a first sight of such a spectacle as war.

We began to climb the slope of the steep
hill towards the sound of the guns. Before we
had gone a hundred yards, I had had to stop
three times to pick the prickles out of my canvas

shoes. Those shoes had seemed so serviceable in Barcelona. One or two more prickles, and we reached the firing-line.

I seemed to have seen it all before, though in what film it was hard to place. It was the most conventional war scene imaginable. We had reached a line of men, who were stretched out on their stomachs on the ground, their guns to their cheeks, while at an interval of every twenty-five yards or so a machine-gun had been planted. Five hundred yards beyond them we could see Monte Aragon. The fortress, which had held out during the whole of the Carlist War and remained unshaken by all previous revolutions, presented its broad, crenelated face to our guns. As we reached the first machine-gun, which was hidden by a high boulder, a long hurrah broke out which wavered over the line of men like wind over corn, and I saw that one of the towers had been blown to pieces.

We were on the crest of the hills, and the fortress rested on the knees of an opposite hill, a valley lying in between. To our left was Huesca, and its lower-lying district had just caught fire from our bombs. Thick plumes of smoke mounted slowly against a blue screen of sky. Three of our aeroplanes winged over the edge of the town, and after their passage a spout of fire sprang up so high that for an instant the clouds were gilded.

Our hill sloped away and back to the left, and there, where the firing line curved back about a hundred yards, the artillery was at work, tirelessly loosing flights of ammunition against Huesca and Monte Aragon. Looking down towards them, I saw the snout of cannon protruding here and there among the trees, and a few figures of men. Suddenly an anti-aircraft gun vomited about an inch (probably 50 yards) away from an aeroplane and left a smoke bubble to float in the air. The aeroplane buzzed on undisturbed.

As we stood near the machine-gun, sheltered by the stone, I saw a stout person strolling along with perfect composure in the firing-line, stopping from time to time to take notes and look through a pair of field glasses.

"Is that an enemy 'plane?" I asked him as soon as he came up, pointing at another moving dot which had just appeared in the sky.

"No, that's our little reconnoitring 'plane," he replied, and trained his field-glasses back on to Monte Aragon.

He gave a few brief orders.

"Who is he?" I asked, amazed at so much casual indifference to the danger.

I learned in a minute that it was Pico, of our Executive Committee. Everybody was giving him advice.

"Don't be so careless, Pico, get behind that stone."

"Get down from there, Pico, they can see you from Monte Aragon."

Pico muttered something or other, took down a few more notes, and, obedient like a big child, got down behind the stone.

An aeroplane flew past, swooping down so low that we could hear the pilot calling out to us that the electric plant of Huesca had been hit.

The sergeant of the machine-gun section was a German Jew. We stood chatting to him until it was time to relieve the posts. He did not have far to go to find the men who were to take over. They were there already, lying asleep on the ground, one by each gun ready to take his turn. There were two men to every gun, and one fired for four hours while the other slept, and then they changed. They had been like that for five days and nights, without stopping, without ever moving away from their posts.

The sergeant went up to each man in turn, and touched him in a friendly way on the shoulder, or lifted his head in his hands, and said in his strong, gutteral Spanish:

"It's your turn now, comrade."

The men crawled up immediately, like sleep walkers, and took the guns, and their predecessors fell asleep instantly.

I shall never forget the face of utter fatigue on a Catalan boy, almost a child, the lids of his blue eyes swollen and red with the strain, who could not wait for the sergeant to come and wake up his partner, and how he dropped the gun and rolled over on to his side, like a bundle of something broken, and slept.

I did not wait for the sergeant, either. I seized the place the boy had left and threw myself face downwards in line between the two sleepers. Resting on my elbows, I pressed the butt of the gun against my shoulder and fired the first real shot I had ever fired in all my life.

We slept that night rolled up in rugs on the side of the mountain, and it was certainly not the next day that we were to have our grand meal in Huesca.

One of the characteristics of the revolution at the front in the golden age of the Anti-Fascist Militia Committee was a complete absence of the militarist spirit—as stupid as it is necessary. For that reason, the sound of a bugle blowing at the unprecedented hour of 8 a.m. aroused from us all the most energetic protests. The only excuse for such a bugle call was a pressing attack of the enemy. As the enemy seemed to be nowhere at hand, once the first moment of alarm had passed and we found ourselves safe, a huge murmur of resentment began, which looked as though it would be slow in dying.

"The bugle, indeed! I say, comrade lieutenant, is the King coming to review us, by any chance?"

"And me, who ran away from home in South America so as not to do my military service!"

A very dreamy young man, his long hair under his militia cap looking like a perfect nest for the muses, remarked: "I believe there was once a revolutionary writer who wrote a whole book about the right to laziness. We're only asking for the right to rest."

"Now, listen to me, comrade poet," said our lieutenant, with some energy, "it's no use you making anarchist verses here. You've chosen the wrong place for resting this time. Just have a look over there. See them? Well, those 'planes are Fascist."

"And is that what you woke us up for? As though we'd never seen a 'plane before."

We threw ourselves down again under the shadow of a tree, trying to catch up with the sleep which had eluded us.

I felt bruised all over. My hip-bone seemed to have been boring into the mountainside all night, and my bones ached to the marrow. I had never before realised how hard the earth can be.

Suddenly there was another bugle-call. This time we were all on our feet in one act, our mess-kits in our hands. A man was leading a line of mules up the slope towards us, and they were loaded with provisions. We gathered round him when he stopped by the ambulance, which was camouflaged under some trees about 200 yards back from the firing line.

"How many?" the muleteer asked.

The lieutenant began counting us.

"Let's see. How many are we? There are ten in the ambulance, and how many more of you are here? Seventeen . . . nineteen . . ."

"And twenty. Don't forget me," Mercedes
called out, waving to catch our attention.
She had moved off a short distance from us,
and was squatting with her trousers down and
her bare buttocks shining very white in the sun.

We all helped the provisioner, who gave us
our portion of an omelette of 800 eggs.

The eggs gave rise, of course, to all the obvious
Spanish puns, of which the women comrades
were the butt as well as poor comrade Isidor,
with his long tapering neck and too pale hands.

"All the same," a militia-man said thoughtfully, his mouth full of bread and egg, "it
would be more revolutionary to stop all the
ragging and treat the women as though they
were our equals."

"Yes, he's quite right. We must just treat
them as real comrades, and nothing more."

"Oh, but why?" protests Remedios, stopping
with her mouth open and her fair, untidy hair
flying round her face, "I don't want to be
treated as if I wasn't a woman. I took a man
before I took a gun."

The day seemed as though it would be calm.
We left the others in our sector and set out
alone. There was little movement. We had
not much difficulty in getting from one of our
outposts to the next. We were going to Tierz,
and went along, dodging behind the clumps of
trees to avoid the shots on the way, and trying
to make ourselves very small and thin and
quick at the uncovered places.

Tierz is the last little village before reaching
Huesca, hanging to the hem of Monte Aragon's
skirts. By going in a straight line from where
we set out it could be reached in ten minutes
on foot. However, a straight line would have
taken us past Monte Aragon which, although
we had already taken it from the Fascists in
our press, was in actual fact to wait a week
longer before our militias ratified the news.
The only way, therefore, of reaching Tierz,
was to go down to the main road to Barbastro,
from there go up to La Granja—follow on to
Ballesta, and from there Tierz would be about
a couple of hours away at a walking pace.

On the road we saw a car and stopped it.

"Is this the right way to Tierz?"

The three men looked out at us, the chauffeur
with his long sallow face, and two passengers,
one of whom was also dark and, like the chauffeur,
obviously not Catalan and the other thin and
young with light eyes set flush with his face.

"We were going to ask you the same thing,"
the chauffeur said. "Hop along in and we'll
try to get there all together."

The dark man opened the door for us without
a word, and a few minutes later we reached La
Granja de Huesca. La Granja had just been
taken by Colonel Villalba and the Montana
Cuidad de Rodrigo battalion No. 4. As we
stopped the car to ask the way again, I got
out for a moment to ask Villalba for details for
the newspapers. He had fallen asleep like a

log, on the spot, two hours after La Granja
had been conquered.

"May I take your picture?" I asked him,
when I had woken him up. I had a camera
which they had given me for my reporting.

"Willingly," he said courteously, hiding the
fact that he was very tired, "but on one condition." He smiled, and put out his arm to
touch the shoulder of a swarthy man who was
standing by. "That is that when you write
about us in the papers you won't forget to
mention this chap. His name is Andres Mas,
and they call him the Black Cat. You'll be
hearing about him, and all they say about
his courage and the deeds he has done is true."

I promised not to forget the Black Cat.

"At what time did you take La Granja?" I
asked.

"We took it at nine o'clock in the morning."

"How long did the battle last?"

"We had begun fighting at six o'clock in
the morning."

"Many dead?"

"Not a great many."

I went back to the car and found my
companions in difficulty. A militia-man was
telling them:

"You won't be able to take the car any further
than Ballestar. From there on it's a plain, and
the car would be a perfect bull's-eye. You've
got the enemy on all sides of you."

The two men in the car were doctors, and

the back of the car was full of medical equipment and supplies.

At last one of the guards suggested:

"You'll have to carry as much as you can yourselves, and go on foot, and have a mule sent over at night with the rest. '*Salud,*' comrades. Don't forget," he added to the chauffeur, "take the second track to the right."

"Yes, I know."

We bowled off.

Our conversation took on a general interest concerning a little pile of ashes which we passed on the side of the road, with a partially burned crucifix, which the fire had not managed totally to destroy, sticking up out of it. This was all that remained of the priest of La Granja.

"Don't you think we may have passed the turn off for Tierz?" the sombre doctor demanded suddenly.

We knew that La Granja was only two miles from Huesca, but coming round a bend in the road we saw Huesca so near to us that, although we were all aware of what town it was, we couldn't help asking each other:

"That can't be Huesca, can it?"

There was nobody to ask this time. There was only a waste of solitude and the silence of the sun. Our throats went dry when, 250 yards away, a sharp fusillade proved that we had overshot the turn. We swallowed hard and went back, burning the road with our hasty tyres.

Nothing tickles the appetite like a nervous shock, and the dinner we ate in Ballestar, having finally found the path, was certainly one of the best I have eaten in all my life. None of us were able quite to get rid of a nervous and somewhat childish giggle, which pursued us throughout the meal, and throughout the time we spent after it, drinking the new wine of the district.

"I feel just like a convalescent," the young doctor said, his light eyes seeming paler. I felt the simile to be well chosen, even if he had said it because he was a doctor.

By the time the meal was over, we felt we had known each other all our lives. The chauffeur was particularly unbending, possibly because he came from Andalucia.

"Ha, ha, comrade," and "he, he, comrade," was chiefly what his conversation amounted to, clapping me vigorously on the shoulders. "Ho, ho, comrade, that was the wrath of God for having laughed at the burnt priest."

"You'll be able to write it all up in the newspapers."

"What a scoop."

I felt I had lived a good half column.

VIII

TIERZ

(Narrative by Juan Bred)

WE WERE ALREADY PREPARED TO SET OUT ALONE
for Tierz, in spite of the danger and the fact
that we did not know the road. Our comrades
seemed to have been overcome by their lunch.
They had wandered away afterwards to sleep,
and now it was already four o'clock in the
afternoon and none of them had shown up.
We determined to start off, and were walking
down the street when I suddenly saw them
coming along, yawning, and with their eyes
still half shut. They were profuse in excuses,
especially the chauffeur.

We began to walk to Tierz, each of us piled
up with as many of the medical supplies as we
could carry. The captain of the column which
was occupying Tierz joined us. He was also bound
for the same place and proposed to walk along
with us. We were very glad of this, and joyfully
loaded his broad back and chest with as many
parcels as we could persuade him to carry. He
made us take our guns with us, too, against the
danger, and this made the trip very heavy going.

We walked out of Ballestar, walking directly towards Monte Aragon. The castle surged up at us, seeming very near now, and the little road appeared to be bringing it on top of us. The path, which still bore traces of a plough, went up and down, dipping and rising, and was sometimes bordered by low bushes behind which, by bending a little, we could feel ourselves in comparative safety. We went along in Indian file, and when we came to the open spaces which offered no protection the captain, who was ahead, speeded up the pace. At the same moment a few bullets began to fly.

After some seconds of this, I asked:

"You don't think those are aimed especially at us, by any chance, do you?"

To which the dark, gaunt doctor replied in a world-weary tone:

"When you've had as much of the front as I have, my young friend, you'll be used to this sort of thing."

All the same, he looked pale.

Eventually we reached a plantation of maze and there we felt a little more sheltered. Ahead of me, I could hear the captain telling something to the chauffeur:

"It's the little priest."

"What's that about a little priest?" I asked.

"It's the priest of Heusca who was trying to pot us. He's a most unrepentant huntsman. He winged five of our men this week already in the little spot we've just crossed. But he can

G

only hit a target if people are walking in a group, because he's shooting at 500 metres. I know all about the business from a prisoner we took this morning. It appears that this priest perches himself up in one of the trees of that little copse every day, with his gun and his pipe and enough ammunition and tobacco to last the day. They bring his food to him, and I hear that he's even built a little platform in the tree for himself, and a rest for his gun."

We keep on walking towards Monte Aragon. By this time it is only four hundred yards away, and we are very relieved when the path takes a bend to the right and we make our entry into Tierz. It is hidden in a little valley, behind a fold in the ground, and we come upon it suddenly by surprise.

Tierz is a diminutive village, and like all the small villages of Aragon, it is made of stone, and coloured a doubtful white. Two streets present themselves for your selection, but it is needless to hesitate over the choice. They both lead you faithfully to the square in front of the church, which is the centre of the town. On either side of the square, the large, clumsy houses look as if they had been built by children: two holes, a door and a window, and another hole, the chimney, and nothing more.

On every street corner we saw a notice posted up:

"Comrades: keep close to the walls."

"That's because," as the captain explains to

us, "we're easily seen here from Monte Aragon which overlooks the village."

Before reaching the church square, we cross four or five little streets which pass us with an abrupt, clear white sweep down to the river. The church has been burned, and in the square a nymph continues to blow water out of a vague hole in her face. At this fountain, as at fountains all over the world, a group of children were playing, splashing water at each other.

As we reached the square, a strange sight caught my eye. Two women were walking towards us, pressed close in the lea of the houses, swathed in splendid dressing-gowns and their feet in embroidered slippers.

"Those are two 'international' comrades," the captain hastened to explain to Mary. "One is French and the other Swiss. You must get to know them, because the Swiss girl speaks such good English."

When the presentations were done, we found that one was a militia woman, and the other a nurse, the wife of an Italian anti-Fascist who was chief of a patrol.

"We're off for a bathe," the Swiss girl said to us in English. "Will you come along, too? I think there are still one or two dressing-gowns left among the things we requisitioned in the Mayor's house."

It was very hot, and we had to decline with regret.

"We're so busy. We have to go and declare

ourselves at the People's Committee. But we could go down to the river with you just for a minute, to have a look."

"Yes, do," she said, taking Mary's arm.

"Is it far?" I asked.

"No, we're almost there."

The captain slipped off to interview a batch of prisoners, and we, the two doctors, and the chauffeur went down towards the river with the women.

"I wish I'd known about this before we came," the fair doctor said, with a sigh. "I'd have brought my bathing trunks with me."

Our two new women friends looked at each other and laughed. I wondered why.

I was soon to learn.

We came out suddenly on to the bank of the river. It was full of naked militia-men, leaping about and laughing and throwing water at each other. The sun was sliding and slipping off their shining backs and stomachs, and their legs flashed about like long pale fish in the water. One man was lying on his back in midstream. He began beating the water with his arms and feet until it churned up like whipped cream and spirted at his comrades like soda out of a siphon. They splashed back at him in turn, or ran away shouting. Further along, other slim, bare men were climbing about on each other's shoulders and diving off noisily.

Mary spent a moment of decided embarrassment until we got used to the idea.

For a moment I did not look at the other two women. I could feel them standing beside me on the bank, their brilliant draperies moving in slow, colourful folds in the wind. The men in the water were jumping up and down, waving and calling out to them to come in and join them. Suddenly, they both opened their clothes and threw them away and dashed past me. They went down the bank into the water, their naked bodies glowing an ardent amber colour in the sunlight.

The doctors, the chauffeur, and we two, stood looking at them and waiting there with nothing to say. Only the chauffeur at last recovered something of his Andalusian loquacity.

He tapped me on the shoulder:

"Ha, ha, comrade, there's the revolution for you."

We sat down on the edge of the river.

The Swiss woman came towards us, her arms making curves through the air as she lifted them alternately out of the water, the drops spraying off, and at each stroke half her body rising above the surface, showing her ripe breasts. When she came to where we were, she caught hold of a boulder with both hands, and lay there in the water looking up at us. Her long muscular legs floated out behind her.

She began to talk to us, and we chatted in French.

After a while I couldn't help asking her:

"Doesn't it embarrass you at all?"

"What?"

"Oh, bathing like this in your skin with all those naked chaps."

She broke into a clear, sane laugh.

"Why, whatever for? They're quite harmless. Of course sometimes one or other of them does a little masturbation, but so respectfully that one has really nothing to say."

Suddenly, an intense sound of murmuring filled the air. I looked up. It was going too fast to see the markings on the wings. The machine flew on, disappeared in the direction of Monte Aragon, only to come back flying much lower.

Meanwhile a lively discussion had broken out in the water. Fascist or not? But a big dark boy, with his body burnt brown, rushed up out of the river and began climbing into his trousers.

"Don't talk to me about it," he exclaimed. "That bird's Fascist. I can tell by the sound."

Two minutes later the aeroplane was back again, flying much lower and showing its black wings. Everyone fled out of the water.

I looked round anxiously for a place of refuge and we both began running towards the bridge. I thought we would get under it. As we reached it a wet hand clasped mine and pulled me back.

"Not under there. They know about it. They always aim at the bridges."

It was the Swiss woman. We ran back, all three together, and hid among the trees.

The aeroplane laid a couple of eggs and flew off. Afterwards we heard that they had fallen further away, on the other side of the village, and had injured a child and killed a mule.

I left my companion with the women and I went to declare our arrival at the People's Committee. Among the ungainly houses there was one of gracious build, two storeyed, which had formerly belonged to the Mayor. It belonged now to the People's Committee. I went in. It had all the usual modern conveniences such as running water, and an air of ease and luxury. There was a court behind it, and a terrace hung with vines where wicker chairs stood waiting in the shade.

A militia-man standing guard asked me:

"Are you the journalist comrade who has just arrived?"

"Yes."

"Then the captain has been asking for you. He's upstairs. You'll find him on the second floor."

I went up. At the entrance to a room on the second floor a guard tried to stop me going in.

"No entrance, comrade."

"This is the journalist comrade who has just arrived," the man said who had followed me up the stairs. "The captain asked to see him."

He let me in.

A massive table occupied the centre of the room, which was large, and preciously furnished with carved seventeenth century pieces. The captain was seated at the table, with another man at his side, and two soldiers were standing facing them from across the breadth of the table. These soldiers belonged to a batch taken from the enemy. I came in for the end of the interrogatory.

The captain signed to me to sit down, and went on asking:

"Well, which would you rather do? Go to your family in Barcelona, or join up with our forces and fight?"

"I'd rather fight on your side. I always wanted to, anyway. As I was telling you, I've got my brother on this side as it is, and it was only because I was forced that I——"

"All right, all right, that's enough. Go off downstairs and have a meal."

When the soldiers had gone, the captain turned round to me and presented the man seated beside him as the Political Commissar. We talked, and the commissar explained to me:

"Those are the last two soldiers of the nine we took from the Fascists. We have been judging them to-day."

"What do you mean to do with them?"

"You can see for yourself that we have set them all free. We mean to make sound revolutionaries of them, let us hope. Oh, the soldiers are no problem at all. The problem in this case is an officer and a lawyer whom we have captured. The latter was armed with a revolver when we took him—it was the other day, when we cut off the road to Huesca—but in spite of that we're sending him off to Barcelona to have an enquiry opened about him."

"And the officer? What about the officer?"

The commissar shrugged and shook his head.

"What do you expect us to do with a Fascist officer?" he asked. He seemed a little pre-occupied, and added, tracing a figure in pencil on his block of notes: "The trouble is that he's wounded."

"Wounded, my eye!" the captain said impatiently. "The man's been shot in the leg, that's all. He can walk."

"Still . . ." the commissar said.

"Will you shoot him wounded?" I asked.

The commissar sighed and put up his eyebrows.

"What can we do?" he said, as though with regret. "We can't keep him here. You know what it would be if we sent him to Barcelona. And anyway, prisoners don't exist in a civil war, nobody keeps them, so it has to come to the same thing in the end, sooner or later."

"He can walk, anyway," the captain said.

"All the same, I think we had better not have him come up the stairs for his cross-examination. We'll go and see him at the hospital."

"Yes, yes, of course. Come along, let's go down now," said the captain, rubbing his hands, "then we can eat first. I'm as hungry as a hunter."

We ate all three together, and then I went with them over to the hospital.

The hospital was the old school-house. There were still two or three sums on the blackboard, and rows of beds had replaced the rows of benches in the form-room. Only two people were there —the officer whom we had come to see, and lying dressed on a bed a little further away, a soldier, wounded in the arm, who had been captured from the same regiment.

"Well, how's the leg going along, captain?" the commissar asking, coming in.

The Fascist officer had very black hair and a dark, fattish face. He looked smooth and well-polished, his hair plastered down.

"It's nothing, I assure you," he said. He made as though to get up.

"No, no, don't rise. Don't disturb yourself."

A look of anguish broke suddenly over the polite face.

"Please tell me something," he said hoarsely. "If they are going to kill me, why are they healing me up first?"

The commissar carefully avoided giving a reply to this question.

"Have you had anything to eat yet?" he asked, with courteous concern. The prisoner made a gesture towards a tray which had been pushed back on to a table near the bed, so the commissar went on: "I'm sorry, but I'm afraid we shall have to disturb you for a short while, we have to cross-examine you."

He plunged straight away into the routine questions—age, name, place of birth, regiment, etc. The prisoner replied to everything in a neutral tone.

"To what political organisations have you belonged?"

"I haven't belonged to any. I've always been in the army. I've only tried to do my duty."

"I should have thought your duty would have been to stand by your legally constituted Government," the commissar said, a humorous, ironic smile creeping into the corners of his mouth.

"Yes, but you forget that I was in Saragossa. Perhaps if I'd been in Barcelona I might have been on your side."

"How many men have you now in Huesca?"

"Five thousand."

"Have you enough supplies?"

"More or less."

"Do the troops obey you willingly?"

The captain seemed not able to reply to this, and asked for it to be more clearly put.

"I mean," the commissar said patiently, "aren't you sometimes obliged to use violence to make the soldiers obey you?"

"Sometimes one has to be a little energetic, yes."

"Where is the powder magazine?"

The officer swallowed once or twice. He looked down at the sheet and drew the edge of it along between his fingers. Then his eyes slipped round towards the soldier, who was lying there on the other bed. The soldier's eyes had not left the officer during all the time of the cross-examination.

The commissar felt the strain, and turned round and addressed the soldier:

"How do you feel?" he asked. "Do you feel well enough, say, to get up a bit and leave us alone here?"

As the soldier passed us, going towards the door, we heard him mutter:

"Not much stuffing left in the officer now."

The commissar felt it would have been brutal to return immediately to the attack. So he said:

"Where is your family now? In Huesca?"

"No, in Saragossa."

Then:

"Where is the powder magazine?"

"You know as well as I do, commissar."

"We believe we know. What we want is the certainty."

"It's where it's always been." The officer does not look at us. He ends by giving us the details.

"Why haven't you attacked? You're in a better position than we are."

"How should I know?"

"Do you think you have enough material?"

"Not overmuch."

"Are your aeroplanes of Italian or German make?"

"I hear we have some of both."

The officer's face looked strained and tired round the eyes. He lay back as though worn out.

"Do you think," he asked, picking up a glass of wine from the used dinner-tray, "that I might have this changed for a little water?"

The commissar closed his book.

"I think the captain is tired," he said. "We must see to it that he has some rest."

He opened the door, and called out to the little militia-girl who was on duty to help the nurse in the hospital. Presently she brought in a bottle of water and a glass, and administered to the prisoner, looking conscientious and child-like with her freckled nose and the sleeves of the khaki blouse rolled up to show her fat brown arms.

The officer closed his eyes a second, as though pulling himself together for an effort, and then opened them and asked:

"Are they going to shoot me? Anyway, I want to ask you if you will please be so kind as to send on to my wife and my mother the two letters you allowed me to write to them. And let me thank you for the kindness I have received at your hands. I spoke about it in the letters I wrote, and told them how surprised I was because we always hear that you are vandals who ill-treat and torture their prisoners."

"I don't think you can have believed that. Those are the kind of stories which can only be told to ignorant peasants."

He had no answer to this, and returned to his liedmotiv:

"If I am going to be shot, why am I being cured?"

When we left, the little militia-girl caught us up.

"Are they going to kill him? Poor old chap, I'm sorry for him."

The commissar raised his eyebrows and stared at her in amused astonishment.

"Fancy you saying that! And this morning you were insulting the man and wanting to tear his eyes out."

"This morning he was a Fascist. Now he's only a poor sick thing."

"Dear me," the commissar said thoughtfully, "I'd almost fogotten that he's not such a bad-looking chap."

"It isn't that at all. You know it isn't. And anyway, I don't like tubby men. But I don't want them to kill him."

There was nothing the commissar could say. So he tweaked her nose affectionately, and we went away.

I have never understood for what perverse reason prisoners are shot at dawn. They are allowed to see the beginning of a new sun before they are killed. Perhaps it is to give them the illusion that they have lived a day longer. That particular execution was fixed for five o'clock, and the sun was coming up already behind Monte Aragon when we reached the courtyard.

We waited there, making the best of the excuse which the early cold gave us for shutting ourselves away from the prisoner's gaze inside the folds of our cloaks. He came forward slowly, between two guards, leaning on a cane. He was draped in a blanket.

It was just before they fired that we saw him stagger and seem about to fall. The little militia-girl ran forward to him with one of the wicker chairs, and pushed it behind his knees. This was how it happened that he died seated, and his cane made a long rattling slap as it rolled over and over towards us down the gentle slope of the stone paving.

Afterwards, a day like any other day began. Only there were no birds left any more.

IX

THE CLINIC HOSPITAL

(*Narrative by Mary Low*)

I WENT BACK TO BARCELONA AND WORKED again. Almost every night it was the small hours before I slept. The night was absolutely silent under the windows, only broken once or twice by a whistle blowing to stop a car for inspection.

Once, I had fallen into the heavy sleep of exhaustion when the door burst open and Breá ran in covered with mud and blood and in khaki with his hair flying.

I sat up.

"What is it?"

"It's Robert," he said, coming nearer and panting. He must have run up the stairs. I thought he smelt odd. "He's downstairs in the wagon. We brought him back, we thought it seemed better that way."

"Why?" I tried to see in the sudden glare of the electric bulb. My eyes felt rubbed with sandpaper.

"He's dead."

Robert had been one of our friends, politically and otherwise. He was twenty-two. I remember getting to know him on the first floor of the local when a pile of books had been put out for us to read and everybody was scrambling for them. There was only one that I wanted, Rimbaud's *Une Saison en Enfer* and Robert got it before I did. We quarrelled because he would not give it up.

While I got dressed, Breá who had come from the front explained:

"Fifty of us from the International Column went to capture a house on the main road. Robert was the only one they got. He lay out on the road for hours before we could get back to him. We thought he might be alive still, but he was shot in the head."

It was the first death in the International Column.

The house was still and dark when we went along the corridors and down the stairs, but there was a curious kind of whispering noise everywhere. Somehow it must have filtered round the international dormitories already that someone had died. The noise made it sound as though the building were sighing in its sleep.

It was a full-moon night, and through the glass doors the hall was white. We went out into the Ramblas in front of the local. An open van was standing near, shadowless in the bright clear night. Inside it, four militia-men were standing at the four corners, facing outwards, the bulwarks of the van reaching to their thighs.

H

Their faces were bowed over the guns they held on end before them.

We went slowly up, and a man who was there let down the end edge of the van like a flap. An odd-shaped packet filled the middle space between the four guards, done up in red.

"Would you like to see him? We brought him here before taking him to the hospital so that the comrades should see him."

A number of other people had come out of the local by this time. They stood about on the steps for a moment, and then gathered round. Two militia-men sprang up into the van and began unfolding the red cloth.

I climbed up like the others and went to look.

A stranger, rather dark-skinned, with a big belly, was lying stiffly there. I thought at first it couldn't be Robert.

"He's very changed," somebody said.

"Looks much older."

"Far gone already."

Robert's face was turned away over his shoulder, with an expression of surprised pain round the mouth, and his two fists were clenched and lifted tightly towards his heart. I began to be able to identify him.

"Look at the hole in his head."

Stelio, the Italian doctor, squatted down on the floor of the van and put his forefinger into the wound. It went in its whole length.

"I can just feel the bullet now," he said. "It's lodged at the base of the skull."

We stood round stricken and did not speak
any more. Some of the people who had climbed
up into the van were new "internationals" who
had come fresh from their countries and had
never known Robert. They would be going out
to the front in a new group. Some of them were
young and had never seen death before.

Presently the ambulance drew up, and we
transferred the body into it on a stretcher and
ourselves followed to the hospital in a car. It
was the Clinic Hospital which included the
Morgue, and we drove a long way to reach
it.

We drove into a cobbled court. Beyond
that was the building, which looked like a
barracks with its many windows and bald front.
A line of steps led down into the stone-vaulted
basement, and I followed the men who were
carrying the stretcher down it.

A gust of formol met me and then we were
in a big room, with piles of people spread casually about on long tressel tables, or on the floor.
Blood and water was running down the sloping
floor into a grating.

At first I couldn't believe they were real people.
I went from one to another and stared. They
looked like lay figures, just as stiff and the same
colour. Now I know, I thought, why wax
models always look so inhuman—they're copied
off the dead and they really look like them.

There was a man lying near the door, with
a haughty expression on his face, the grey hair

sweeping back in a mane from his forehead, and his nose thin and curved. Another whose face struck me was a little man, who seemed to sleep, his cheek nestled down into his shoulder. He, and a fat man on the floor with his legs flung out sideways as though he were dancing, were the only ones who seemed a little real.

Some of them had no faces.

Two or three men were on guard, and helped us to lay Robert on the end of one of the tables, though it seemed awful to leave him there. We talked to them about all the bodies.

"Some of them have been brought back from the front," one of the guards said, "and most of the others are spies or Fascists. We are always discovering some who are hidden away. We put up their photographs on the wall outside the hospital, to notify anybody who wants to claim them, but people are afraid of acknowledging those kind of friends and relations."

He took me up into the courtyard again, and by the light of a lamp showed me rows of photographs of every kind of dead body which were tacked up on the wall under a pillared arcade. I longed to ask him why they all had their shoes and stockings off, but did not dare.

One of the militia-men who had accompanied us came up the steps from the basement as we stood talking there and joined us.

"I've just seen another room, with more in it," he explained, "only those in there have grown twice the size."

We had to come back there again the next afternoon, to fetch Robert in his coffin to the cemetery. The party came in large numbers from the local to share in the procession, and the wide court of the hospital in the sunshine was full of herds of people. The building was sand yellow by day.

I was surprised to see guards lined up on the steps of the Morgue, and the people filing down between them into the basement. Robert had been put into another room already. I wondered why they were all going down, and joined the line, forgetting the strange indifference of Spanish peoples to their own death and the powerful attraction that death itself exercises over them.

The Morgue was quite a show that afternoon. Everything had been washed down, and the dead lined up as neatly as possible. The tables had been pulled out from the walls so that one could walk all the way round them and two guards, planted in the centre of the floor, were directing the circulation to the right:

"Pass along this way, please, comrades."

They all passed along, people of every age, and sort, and I saw pairs of very young lovers, holding each other by the hand and going to the Morgue as they might have gone to the zoo.

Some wounded comrades from the International Column were being treated upstairs in the clinic Hospital itself, and I went in to see them. The Arab boy had been shot in the chest, and he lay flat in his bed, his eyes shut and his face an unhealthy dust colour. His breath came out of his open mouth in a rough, whistling way.

Farther along the ward was the Belgian miner, propped up on his pillows, with his arm and one shoulder done up in plaster of Paris. His yellow hair had grown long and untidy.

I went and talked to him.

"How are you?"

"Not too bad. It isn't so painful any more, but it's so uncomfortable."

"You must be fed up."

He grinned.

"Not awfully. You see, they made quite a do at home when I came out here, and all the boys at Charleroi got together and stumped up the money for the fare because they wanted to send someone to represent us miners in the revolution, and of course we're too poor all to come. Of course, I've been sending pictures of me at the front, and all that, but when a chap gets wounded it seems somehow (it's silly of course, because we all run the same risks)—well, it seems as though he's really done something."

I went down into the yard again, and by this time they had got the coffin aboard a hearse with black horses, and we put a big red flag, with "IVth International" sewn on it in white, over the top, and set off in procession. We felt the P.O.U.M. would be annoyed over the flag,

but Robert had been one of us so we didn't
mind if they were or not. The P.O.U.M. is
still talking about a "new" and the "next"
and "another" International, but they haven't
decided on the number yet, and a mention of
the IVth makes them fidget.

Funerals were often used as a jumping-off
ground for political declarations. The procession
would march slowly through the town, the
music ahead playing a solemn lament, and
ourselves following in uniform afterwards,
walking so slow that our ankles trembled, and
then the car, and people carrying wreaths, and
then the crowd. We always wound down the
Ramblas, and stopped opposite the party local,
and suddenly somebody from the Executive
Committee—Gorkin, or Bonet probably—would
spring up on to the roof of the funeral carriage,
and holding out his arms begin to harangue.
The name of the man whose body they bestrode
was only an excuse, of course, to give them an
opening for a political speech. When we took
Robert past the local that day, after Bonet had
spoken, Rous, with his clumsy body, clambered
surprisingly up on to the hearse, and stood
there gesticulating in the wind and rain, a white
paper with some notes on it flapping in his hand
like a handkerchief saying good-bye. He spoke
about the IVth, but the roar of a line of trams
going by behind him swallowed up the words.
Afterwards, it was Benjamin Peret, saying something in French, his thin voice snatched away

by the wind. The day was growing prematurely dark with the storm, and under the rays of an early lamp the circle of Catalan faces were raised towards him without comprehending.

It was over. People ran up and piled the wreaths into a van, and the funeral carriage set off at a smart trot down the last miles to the cemetery. The procession crumbled up and we were alone under the trees.

We went to a café kept by a French woman, in a narrow street off the Ramblas. There were two or three red round tables set out on the strip of pavement. We sat sipping drinks. As night fell, the street, which dipped beyond us, and then rose again higher and higher and further off, was pricked out in light, like a festoon drooping and rising. For a long time the people swarmed by us, singing and laughing, and then thinned down, and finally only one or two passed from time to time down the road.

Suddenly we saw a man running down the edge of the pavement with his arms out and his head thrown back. As he darted across the patch of light thrown by the café, he cried out several times:

"Warning! Warning!" in a voice like a whistle.

A long black car catapulted out of the dark and roared down the street, going flat out, with its mudguards touching the pavement on either side of the road and the noses of two or three guns sticking out of the lowered windows.

We leaped back in time. I can still see Rous, not finding any cover, and the wall blocking his retreat, standing pressed back against the lighted wall of the café. Fat, and in a scarlet shirt and khaki overalls, he made a splendid target. Two or three others were crouching behind their chairs. Breá and I threw ourselves flat down on the ground under the row of little tables, knocking one over.

But the shooting only began when the car had rounded the corner into the Ramblas. We heard a volley echoing among the trees. We ran down the street towards the Ramblas at the double. We had our revolvers, but no guns. The patrols were whistling the car to stop for inspection, and the guns in the car had gone off and the patrols and the militia guard from the local opposite were firing on the car, which was still running.

It stopped suddenly with a jolt, and there was a crash of glass. The windscreen had been hit. The guard from the local were all in the street by this time, and a moving screen of figures was between us and the car. One or two shots more made the high fronts of the houses ring. When we were able to see, the car had become dead and mute, and when the militia-men wrenched open the door of the driver's compartment, the chauffeur fell out sideways and slipped down into the road, and a trickle of blood ran away from the inert body.

Of the two men in the body of the car, one

was dead already and the other, crouching down on the floor with a wounded shoulder while still trying to manipulate a gun, was quickly despatched with shots in the head which reduced his face to red pulp. We pulled out strapped boxes and cases which had been piled up inside the car. Some of them had money inside when we broke them open, and jewellery, and clothes, and old pieces of silver and gold ornaments.

"A bunch of Fascists trying to make a get-away," one of the milita-men explained to me, after we had telephoned to the ambulance to come and take the bodies away to the Clinic Hospital. "There must still be a lot of them hidden away somewhere, of course, and from time to time they make a bolt for it. It used to happen much more often in the beginning than it does now, because I suppose we're eliminating them little by little."

"Do they ever manage to get away?"

He grimaced.

"Just imagine. If the patrols only sight them when they're too far off, and there's no one to head them off like we did to-night. Of course the alarm is signalled through to all guards, but even so, if they're making a good speed they have been known to get out. We generally get them, though."

The ambulance came and collected the dead and drove off. It was all white, and drove very fast with a siren blowing, and a white and yellow pennant streaming out from the roof. The lights of the inner room shone dully through the windows as it fled through the streets.

In the Ramblas a little troop of people had collected round the pools of new blood. They stood talking in loud Catalan in the clear night.

X

FLOOD TIDE

(*Narrative by Mary Low*)

EVENTS, WITH THEIR SEPARATE DETAILS WHICH
had seemed to have no importance when taken
one by one, had been following each other all
this time in a slow crescendo and now the
wave broke.

I well remember seeing the first Catalan flag
hung out from a house and carried in procession. It was striped, and burned like a Bengal
tiger in the midst of our plain red and the black
banners of the F.A.I. We stood silent, showing
our faces of disdain and surprise, until somebody
said:—

"The appearance of that is symptomatic."

The Catalan Left Republicans (E.R.C.) who
were supposedly our allies now in the new coalition government of all parties, gave us a demon-
stration up and down the Ramblas, under a
thin revolutionary disguise, when they drove
along in wagons and cars, their barred flag
plentifully mixed with our red, and stood up
with their clenched fists raised. Their band
played the "Internationale," and "Sons of the

People" as well as their own "Els Segadors."
They felt they had to go carefully. Nobody
cheered.

The dissolution of the Anti-Fascist Militia
Committee, and our inclusion in the Government of the Generality, had given the Spanish
Workers' Party new authority, even though it
had shorn numbers of our revolutionary possi-
bilities of their wings. However, the problem
for the party had been how *not* to take part in
the Government, without, the next day being
declared illegal by the Communists and Socialists in power—the anarchists easily swayed—
and extinguished by main force. We profited
by our material betterment, and began to
requisition with a large hand.

It was a game everybody was playing. Buildings were lying empty and waiting for our use
on all sides. First we took the Catalan bank,
a marble decorated palace on the Ramblas
higher up than our local, and the Executive
Committee settled themselves upstairs in the
new apartments. There was almost a room for
each of them now.

We took other locals in big somnolent streets
in the residential quarter, and a whole string
of private houses here and there for district
assemblies. Sometimes we drove a little outside
the town and took over villas in gardens for
hospitals and homes.

The Fascists had often abandoned their houses

and possessions wholesale, even when they had
not been killed, and their belongings left as
they had used them. One Sunday we went in
cars through San Gervasio and looked through
villa after villa.

I remember one in particular, set back in a
deep, steep garden, the fountains still playing
and cascading down over a maze of ferns.
There were hedges of clipped yew, with statues
of naked bronze fawns, and beckoning white
ladies hidden between the trees, and there were
terraces set down one below the other, each
with its lake and lotus-flowers held up on the
broad green leaves, and slow, scarlet fish. Above
the marble edge of the last lake, stairs ran up to a
balustraded terrace, and beyond it reached the
house draped in Morning Glory.

All the doors were shut and carefully locked,
so that the proprietors must have fled and left
everything untouched by the revolution. One
of our militia-men broke a pane in a long glass
door, and we went in.

It was a little palace, with a square wide hall,
and tapestried walls, the hall going right up to
a pointed dome in the roofs with pink-bottomed
angels flying round it, and the other stories
forming galleries with gilded rails. Everything
was in perfect order, only smelling a little of
dust and dead moths, and the only furnishings
the owners seemed to have taken with them were
the pictures off the walls. Everywhere, these
had been cut neatly out of their frames and must

have been taken away in rolls, and the massive carved frames looked down at us from all the rooms like vacant mouths.

There was little we could take, for the house would stand as it was for a sanatorium. We found some old finery and lace fans, and a gramophone with records of guitar players and Andalucian singers. Somebody played some chords at a sweet sounding piano. I went into one of the bedrooms and lay down on a bed with pillars round it and loops of damask and velvet trailing to the ground, and thought of our militia-men sleeping in it and eating off all the fine plates under glass in the dining-room, and felt a foretaste of their pleasure.

A German girl who was with us, and whom the revolution had swept along here from Sitges, —paradise of Germans—where she had been spending the summers of her exile, ran in suddenly excited with a dusty photograph.

"Look," she said, "this must be the owner, and if so I know who it is. I *thought* there seemed to be something familiar about the façade of the house when we came up, but I couldn't quite place it. But now I know. Why, this man used to come to Sitges to a villa there for week-ends. I remember what a silly fop he was, and he talked to us on the beach one day, and showed us photographs of this house and about half a dozen like it. He said they were all his."

"He must have had some money."

"Oh, they had cars and everything. There

were several of them in the same family, and a house for each one of them all in the same district."

"I wish they'd left some more of their stuff about when they escaped, then."

"No fear. They had a goblet that an old king of Spain had had a drink out of once, and they kept it under glass. Seems kind of silly, doesn't it? That must have been what was in that empty show case in the drawing-room, I suppose. And the pictures. He said they were precious, and they've taken them, too."

"If they took so much junk with them, they must have gone at their ease. They probably got away through one of the Latin-American consulates. Those people must be reaping gold."

I thought of the few hundred extra Cubans who had grown up in Barcelona overnight. They walked about with impunity and had flags on wide brassards pinned to their sleeves. Foreigners, and foreign property were supposed to remain untouched.

Among other things which we took at this time of flourish and general expansion were two printing shops. Besides these, we already had a press and large editorial offices. The entrance was in a dark, narrow street where two guards sat half on and half off the pavement in arm-chairs, balanced as well as they could, and past them a double flight of stairs led up to other doors guarded again by other militia-men. One of them was very old and very slow with only one tooth. He spent a lot of his time wandering about the premises, from the business offices to the editorial department, generally in the way, and if Gorkin or Molins, the heads of the Press, made any remonstrance, he answered by a bit of headwagging and the remark:

"You're young yet, comrades, that's why you're so impatient."

Apart from that, he sat generally in a stiff chair in front of the office door, a pair of steel-rimmed spectacles pushed down on to the end of his nose, spelling out the sentences of a French newspaper very slowly.

The reporters' room, where we worked, was a light-painted oblong, with clear woodwork everywhere. Molins—very short, and egg-shaped, the small mouth under the huge jutting nose making his profile look like an interrogation mark—presided over us at a table by himself, next door to a radio and to two or three deep-seated armchairs. This was where we collected round from time to time to listen to Quiepo de Llano's drunken bouts. One side of the room gave on to a den where Gorkin shut himself off less democratically behind a roll-top desk. He had a curiously impersonal face, like most professional revolutionaries, lacking in the mystery of a private life. When I discovered that he had a wife—and a nice one—and a little boy with jug-handle ears, I was astonished to think of him doing all that, and still could see

I

no indication of it in the round eyes behind his spectacles.

The other side of the room had windows and a gallery overlooking the ground floor where the machines were. The heat came up from below in gusts as one leaned over the rail. It was tiring to keep going up and downstairs to talk to the linotypist, and we had tied a cardboard box on to the end of a piece of string and hauled it up and down.

After a time there were too many of us filling up the newspaper office, so we decided to requisition some bureaux for ourselves. There was a suspect land-agency in a building near the Executive Committee's new offices, and we decided to turn them out and take over the premises.

I was not there for the beginning of the business, and arrived only when we were half settled in. All our people were rushing from room to room, struggling in an exuberance of good humour over the distribution of the desks. In the entrance hall, in one of the darker corners, I saw two or three little men of the clerking type huddled together. They had not dared to take off their coats and waited dumbly there.

I went up to them and asked them what they wanted.

"The director sent us," one of them piped up at last, "to see to the final arrangements. But the new people who have taken the office haven't given us time to do any of the checking.

All they've said is that we have to get all our things—all the books and everything,—out of here by to-morrow. And we—we can't, don't you see?" he said, stretching his arms out in a weak, resigned gesture to the piles of junk which had been pulled out of the drawers and littered the tables and chairs everywhere. "How can we, without a van? And you know what the manager's like, he wouldn't hear of it. Besides," he said, his little voice getting higher and crosser, "none of this is in order at all. Most irregular."

"Never mind what the manager says. We can get you a van as soon as you like if only you'll promise to scrape all this stuff together and get it out of the way by to-morrow morning. We really must start work here by to-morrow, and ours isn't the sort of work that waits."

"But it isn't in order. And the checking——"

I was much too optimistic in those days, and as I rang up the local to have them send a van round I thought with delight that this was the end of all red tape, and of all waiting in ante-rooms and suffering managers. Bureaucracy is not got rid of as easily as all that. I learnt soon enough.

The van came, but the little men could not make up their minds to use it without an order from their boss. We were quite patient, and left the empty van waiting for them in the road until the late afternoon, while they still stood turning their hats round in their hands and whispering. In the end, we were obliged to take their stuff for them and start putting it down into the street. Everything was all over the pavement.

One of the American comrades, who was rather sentimental, said to me: "Poor little Fascists, it does seem a shame. Of course I'm all against them, but it's somehow easier on paper. Somehow it makes me feel kind of bad to see them looking like that while we treat 'em rough."

Several self-important fat business men came and went towards evening. They conferred in corners and looked at us hatefully and fearfully. Next day we were already installed, working, and a comrade was painting up the party name in large glittering letters on all the doors.

Much later, after the trip to Madrid and just before the Spanish Workers' Party was put out of the Council of the Generality by the Communist Party, we requisitioned the Virreina Museum. It was an old palace, standing among the other houses towards the end of the Ramblas, but pushed back from the street, and staring down with an aloof, decaying face at the booth-keepers who blocked its entrances. Under the curved vaults upon which it was built a market had grown up, bundles of cheap clothing flapping in the draught; piles of china ornaments, cakes, sweets; and scrubbing brushes and sausages hanging from the ceiling. Somewhere, wedged back in the dark between two stalls, an old-fashioned lift like a boat waited to take passengers up to the other stories. A dim haze of glory had waxed slowly round the Virreina, born of the fact that it was a private museum —which gave it a noble distinction—and that so few people seem ever to have visited it. We were given to understand that it was a precious vial.

We were astonished when we took it over. It contained almost nothing but hideous paintings and thousands and thousands of books, nearly all of them stiflingly dull. The high rooms were full of dust. I longed to disencumber the walls at once and let some fresh air into the rooms. We walked round, measuring the area, and talking about installing an institute for Marxist culture and a club.

"All we have to do is to sort out all the books that are any good, and stack all these pictures and junk in the cellars, or make a bonfire with them."

I encountered unexpected opposition.

"H'm. You know, we don't want to lay ourselves open to any of that stuff about 'revolutionaries destroying treasures of art' and so forth, and you know all the things the Stalinists would love to say about us if they got a chance."

"How could anyone want to clutter up this lovely building with those ugly things? We've got the courage of our convictions, I hope. What's it matter what they say? One doesn't have to respect something simply because it's old."

"Still, the Virreina——"

Nobody could quite get away from the magic which the mention of the Virreina automatically produced. Days and even a week or two later, when plans for an institute had all been drawn up, and material made ready and people nominated for posts, I met a hasty and harried Ros in the dinner queue, his beret crammed down like a battered cake over his ears, and his eyes swimming wearily behind his spectacles.

"Oh," he said, with a sigh of disgust, "don't talk to me about the Virreina. Things are just as they were, and we haven't been able to clear anything out so far. Every day we wait for the photographer to come, and there's always a hitch."

"The photographer? What do you want the photographer for?"

"Well, because the only way out we've been able to think of is to have him come and photograph every room in the place just as we found it, before we move anything. Then we'll have all the documents of the place as proof, and we'll have them reproduced in the press for everybody to see. That way we'll always be able to say: there you are, see, that's the Virreina as it was, and that's all there was to it, and then nobody'll object to us doing what we like with the museum stuff."

"It seemed to me a lot of bother for nothing. After all, you can just stack everything away in perfect safety, if you want to keep the stuff, but out of sight."

Ros shrugged tiredly.

"Oh, you never know. It's better to have everything in order so that they can't have any suspicion of destruction."

I laughed suddenly.

"Ros, you ass, get on with it and hang the photographer. If the Stalinists come into power we'll be bumped off in any case."

We all worked very hard at this time, and sometimes in the Catalan night, rich and blue with the moonlight shining like a blade between the roofs, we walked back to the local at three or four o'clock. It was getting cooler, and we had leather jackets with zip fasteners to replace our summer kit. Sometimes Nin was there, though we saw him rarely since he became Minister of Justice, and now he walked along with us on his stumpy legs down the narrow streets, and carried a portfolio and did not wear militia-clothes any more. His curly hair was hidden by a beret, and he looked grave and owl-like and talked too optimistically. Presently he began to be a hostage, a kind of prisoner in the Generality, and the other parties pulled the strings to see if the figure would work.

Coll called at the newspaper office at night sometimes, too, and walked back with us to the local. He had become one of the heads of the police service now, and we had almost forgotten that he used to wear rope-soled shoes.

Coll had come into possession of the Arch-bishop's car. He drove in it proudly, even for the shortest distances, sitting alone at the back while a chauffeur drove him. When we came down the stairs from the office, we could see the car waiting and taking up all the width of the road. It was lined with purple velvet, even on the floor.

"Come along, Coll, we're all going to walk home."

"But I've got the car here. What do you expect me to do with it? I must drive in it."

"No, come on. We'll walk."

"But my car——"

"Have the car follow us. You've had enough of driving in it. It'll give you a new sensation to have the archbishop's car following you around like a dog."

Coll laughed. He had strong yellow teeth and looked horsey.

The main promenade of the Ramblas was white in the moonlight and almost empty. In the soft night we sat grouped on yellow-painted iron chairs, smoking and listening to a whisper of leaves. Once or twice sailors passed us, going towards the port, with their arms linked and the wide ends of their trousers flapping. We talked about the situation and the line of action, and turned it inside out, and examined even the seams. A group of militia-men with a guitar came and stood some way off under a plane tree. They sang a sardana, their voices rising and falling along the perfect arcs of the music, and one man danced a heel-and-toe Catalan dance. He was slow and graceful, and his body remained quite still and rigid while he danced, and only his legs moved. He snapped his fingers together with a loud cracking noise, keeping time with the steps.

From time to time the patrols passed in groups of three, their guns on their backs. Once they asked us for our papers. When they saw it was one of the heads of the police, they seemed surprised. One of them asked:

"Why aren't you asleep?"

Coll was always late at his post in the mornings.

By degrees, the night came to an end. The dawn would be there before we had finished talking, and so it was already time to start working again.

In those days it often happened that we forgot to go to sleep at all.

XI

MADRID BEFORE THE BOMBARDMENT
(*Narrative by Juan Breá*)

I SET OUT FOR MADRID BY THE NIGHT TRAIN, with my knapsack on my back and my thin summer uniform, for in Barcelona it was still warm. The train was full of men from the militias, and we sat with our elbows touching or stood shoulder to shoulder in the corridors and talked and sang songs. It was dark and the light reached us only at the stations.

Edging along from my compartment into another, I bumped into a Frenchman and began chatting with him. He was a reporter from a newspaper in sympathy with the revolution, and after infinite trouble had managed to get a safe-conduct through Fascist territory. He told me all he had seen.

"I saw the Requetes (Carlists) at mass," he said, "it's extraordinary, after being here, more than worlds away. And I went to see the aviation camps, to look into the question of German aid."

"And were there as many Germans as they say?"

He flung up his hands.

"Ouff! You've no idea. They're settled there as though they owned the place, they've got an entire aviation camp all to themselves quite apart from the Spaniards. They have their own command, outside the domain of the Spanish officers. They've even got their delegates on the General Staff. And, mind you, there's nothing hole-and-corner about all this, it's openly recognised, because they even push their effrontery as far as wearing their Hitler uniforms in public."

"And the Italians? What about the Italians?"

"The Italians are rather a different matter. They're mixed up in the same camps as the Spaniards, and they fraternise with them a good deal, whereas with the Germans there's no contact at all. It's funny, Salamanca's full of German songs at night—'Horst Wessel Lied' and so forth, and the beer flowing as though one were at Munich. It's real Munich beer, too."

I sat down on the same bench with the French journalist for the rest of the night, and we fell into nodding bouts of sleep, and talked together in the intervals. In the morning, at about nine o'clock, it was Valencia, and he got out and left.

The station was full of smoke and the smell of stale trains. I had to change for Madrid, and got out and walked about the platforms. Trains were leaving in all directions for the front. They were full of militia-men. One train had just come in from Madrid. I saw little knots of people waiting to meet it—families, I suppose —who gathered round in anxious tenderness while stretchers were passed through the windows, held as horizontal as possible, and then lowered at a very gentle slope on to the quay. The men lying in them, with their faces and throats swathed tightly up, or else their arms or legs strapped into rigid positions, made clumsy gestures towards those who had come to fetch them. Somewhere in another train I could hear the "Internationale" and "Sons of the People" pouring out full tilt from dozens of deep throats, their separate tunes competing with each other. But the rivalry only ended in cheers and bursts of laughter.

From time to time one of the trains roared out. Sometimes there were women who ran the whole length of the platform, holding on to a hand outstretched out of a window. I saw one young girl, very child-like still, with coils of hail rolled into big ringlets on her neck, decide suddenly to go to the front, too, with the militiaman who was chaffing her from the steps of the carriage. She leaped up beside him, just as the train began to move out, and flung her arms round his lean body. Her mother and father ran beside the train, dragging at her dress to hold her back, and panting, and just as the train finally left the station the thin, dark boy lifted her down to them, and she cried out as though she had been torn.

The train which had come from Madrid was emptying by degrees, but a concentrated group of people was waiting near the van, and I strolled up to see. Some men were lifting down a coffin with a red and black flag thrown over it. When they raised it on their shoulders to carry it down the platform, in spite of the agitation reigning throughout the station a sudden moment of dead silence struck from platform to platform. The long moment seemed to have no end, till a voice broke out from one of the trains: "Down with Fascism!" Everyone echoed the cry, and in a second the whole station was roaring, and the voices sounded thick and rough with indignation and pain. The coffin was moving slowly towards the exit. Even the people following it with flowers and tears had joined in the cry.

My train came in and I entered it. I was in a carriage full of Spaniards from the province of Albacete, and from Sevilla, and we soon got deep into conversation. When lunch-time came, they got out packets of food—some sort of pasty and cold omelette—and handed me a fair share of it. I tried to object and hand it back to them, but the conversation flowed on and over me, without admitting my protests, and as they took so little notice and so much for granted, I ended by resigning myself and eating heartily.

We drank, too. They had two or three leather bottles, full of wine. You held one up in both hands and squeezed it, and a thin spray of wine sprang out from the nipple and entered your mouth. The old leather of the bottles smelt like Don Quixotte's inn.

I had a seat near the window and watched the scenery. After we left Valencia the plain was sprinkled with small swelling hills. From time to time we came to a village, where they sold us a local paper, a young green fruit of the revolution, with a highly coloured title. As everywhere else, the peasants had not grown used to the sight of a passing train, and they stood about to watch us go by, and remembered just in time to put up their clenched fists. Once a cow got on the rails. We were thrown into each other's laps by the sudden stop, while the scream of brakes ripped the air, and the cow stood there for a few seconds longer, switching at the flies with her tail, and then strolled casually away. We all hung out of the windows as we passed her, and yelled out insults as if she had been human. However, she did not even turn her head to look.

We reached Madrid by night, and it was a characteristic arrival. Every country has its peculiarities. On reaching London, a shabby but infinitely respectable Strube's Little Man, complete with bowler, generally offers to sell you *The Times*. In Paris, it is a flower-girl, more faded than her roses. But when you arrive in Madrid, a gaunt and sallow man suddenly unbuttons his coat at you and shows you a belt full of knives, with the remark: "Albacete razors."

It was dark when I left the station, and the town seemed to have been swallowed into a black gulf. I was surprised for a moment, remembering the brilliant lights of Barcelona. Then I remembered how near the front we were. I was in a town at war, and only a dark blue lamp here and there showed in the darkness. As in Barcelona, there were no taxis, and I wondered how to find the local of the Spanish Workers' Party.

I had heard that the party here was small, and had an idea that it would probably amount to something like the official Communist Party in most Latin American countries—that is to say, three comrades and a mimeographic machine. I knew the name of the street where the P.O.U.M. was, of course, but wondered if anyone would know the local and be able to direct us to it.

I asked a man:

"Where is the calle Pizarro, please? That is, we want to get to the local of the Spanish Workers' Party, if you know what part of the street it is in."

"Yes, of course," he said readily, "only it's rather a long way off. But that van standing over there belongs to the Spanish Workers' Party, and if you ask they'll probably drive you."

So we had a van in Madrid. I swelled with pride.

I went over to the van driver.

"Are you going to the party, by any chance? I want to get there, and as I don't know Madrid——"

"I'm not going, as a matter of fact, but jump up and we're sure to meet one of our other vans or one of the party cars which'll take you."

So the party in Madrid was not small after all. My experience of struggling revolutionary groups in other countries had led me to a wrong estimate of what small meant in Spain.

The local was on the second floor of a business building. A guard was outside on the pavement on duty, and in front of them, in the road, a whole string of cars was lined up, their smooth surfaces punctured with "Long live Trotsky," and "Long live the permanent revolution," in red paint. My eyes swelled in their sockets and I felt a heart-beat of astonished delight. I would never have seen that in Barcelona. The party in Madrid seemed definitely to make up in quality what it lacked in quantity.

A short conversation with various comrades made me realise that, in any case, the numbers were not negligible. They talked about various other locals in the town, of their "Lenin" column which was about to leave for the front, of their weekly newspaper, *P.O.U.M.*, of their broadcasting station, and of 900 peasants who would be arriving at our barracks on the morrow. They talked about all this so seriously that I began to think it must be true.

Julio Cid took me to the barracks the next

day. He was strong and hoarse, like all the men fresh back from the front, and full of enthusiasm, revolvers, cameras, and notebooks. He seemed to be good at everything, but this time he had made a mistake which the Supplies Committee were not likely to forgive him in a hurry, since having been sent out to recruit five hundred comrades he had brought back nearly twice the number. However, the Supplies Committee had, after all, not forgotten the miracles of the loaves and fishes. When we reached the barracks 900 peasants were lunching merrily.

The barracks was an old convent. There were two stories and the walls were decorated with painted texts and scrolls, to which the militia-men had added their comments. The building ran round a vast courtyard. The new peasant comrades began to be lined up in this, learning their first military exercises, while others were still giving in their names.

A man stood up on a chair and called out:

"Will all those who can play any musical instrument or know anything about music please come over here with me."

A number of people detached themselves and stood grouped round him, looking eagerly up at where he dominated gesticulating on top of the chair and scanning the horizon of heads for further recruits. I followed him when he climbed down and led the way along to a store-room full of medley of things like a village shop. Everything that had been requisitioned recently

K

was piled about the floors and on shelves in the walls. There was tinned foods and a top hat and books and the robes of a priest and mantillas, and great stacks of music and musical instruments confiscated wholesale from a shop. The latter were to form the equipment of the band.

As we all trooped into the small room, clamouring for trombones and drums and a clarinette, and some complaining because they could only play the guitar, the man who had brought us and who was handing out the instruments told us:

"We've got to form the band. You must hurry up and learn because things are beginning to look rather bad near Toledo."

Nearly all these peasants had come from Extremadura. Their one idea was to take a gun and go back to revenge the death of a brother or an old mother. When, after dinner, we began, as we always did with the regiments, to hand round postcards so that everyone would be able to write home during the campaign, I shall not forget the tone of bitter sadness in which many of them asked us:

"Whom can we write to? Where?"

"Well, to your families."

"But how are we to know if there is anyone still left alive at home, now that the village is in the hands of the Fascists? We've been waiting to be called up by the Government for weeks, but the order never came through. It's the

P.O.U.M. at last, that's given us a chance to do our duty."

"Do you think, comrade," some of them would ask us anxiously, "that we'll soon get given a gun? We'll give them back again, but give us a gun quick, any sort'll do, we're not particular. . . ."

"Don't you worry," we told them, "you'll soon have a good, sound rifle each, and there's no question of having to give them back. They'll be yours for always, for you and your villages, because now the arms belong to the people."

We were lodged at one of the locals of the party, the ex-house of a Count in the Plaza de Santo Domingo. The house had not changed much. On the outside, a large placard announcing: "This local has been requisitioned by the P.O.U.M." was pasted over the place where had been the escutcheons of the Count of Puñoenrostro (literally translated, Lord Fist-in-face). A militia-man in blue overalls with fixed bayonet had taken the place of the liveried footman. Apart from that, there was little that had been altered. Notices had been stuck up here and there: "Editorial Committee"; "To conquer or die"; "Unto the end"; but nothing had been taken away.

The library contained a collection of thousands of books. When I arrived two comrades had been given the work of cataloguing them all. That room, and all the rooms which I explored, remained still almost as his lordship must have left them, full of little useless objects encumbering the furniture and the corners, because we had not had time yet to start clearing up. If it had not been for the noise which went on day and night, with the interminable tapping of manifestos, one might easily have mistaken this splendid house where perfect order and superfluous comfort reigned hand-in-hand with the sickle and the hammer decorating the walls for a mansion of one of the officials of Stalinist bureaucracy in Moscow.

"Come on," said Clara, in whom the militia uniform had not managed to slay her feminine curiosity, "let's look through all the drawers. I want to see what sort of things they had."

She began to be very busy, her hay-coloured hair shooting in and out of cupboards. She was a tall Swiss woman, who had been for a long time in one of the sectors on the Aragon front. We had seen her when she came back to Barcelona for a few days' leave, a tall, thin figure slouching round in blue militia overalls and a check neckerchief, and generally an old cap crammed on to the back of her head.

"It was a quiet sector," she explained to me. "Most of the time it would have been all right, if it wasn't for the dust. Standing guard outside was frightful, when the wind blew, and we all had to take our turn. One daren't turn away and cover one's head even for a moment because we were always expecting a surprise attack, and your eyes got so full of sand and bloodshot and it was heck."

"How did you sleep?"

"Oh, we slept in straw and it was quite comfortable. Fairly clean and not too prickly. It was in a kind of barn."

"And the men?" She had been the only woman in that place and only saw her husband from time to time, as he travelled up and down the front on journalistic jobs.

"The men are all right. They try it on a bit at first, just to see what you're like, but they soon fall in if you're the right sort. Half of them are only kids, anyway. We got along famously."

She gave the impression of being game, of not caring, and lifted her chin, throwing back her thin, pale profile into relief against the dark woodwork of the room.

"Look," she said, and unbuttoned the top of her militia blouse and pushed out a hard shoulder. She showed me a dark blue mark like a stain in the curve of it. "That's what a woman gets from firing at the Fascists, day in day out, when she's not used to it. I had one of those 'musquetons.' They're much lighter to carry than a rifle when you're springing about, but what a kick they've got to them!"

"I suppose you get used to it in time."

"Oh, yes. I'm not a bad shot at all now."

She always had the end of a cigarette stuck to her lip, even when talking. We went back to looking through the drawers of the Count's house.

We found rosaries, and Carlist emblems, and medallions of Saint Barbara the patroness of gunners, with the image of the holy cross and the cannon engraved on both sides, a worthy symbol of catholic ethics. We found every kind of other thing besides. There were love letters, forgotten in the hurry of the flight, and a delicate pyjama in which the soft perfume of the lady of the house still lingered, and the trace of her slim body. There were scarves in which Clara fancied herself, and handkerchiefs as large as little table-cloths with deep borders of lace. There was an infinite variety of other objects which we found, some of them for such special uses that in spite of every effort of our joint imagination, we could not solve the mystery of their use.

XII

A LAST SIGHT OF TOLEDO

(*Narrative by Juan Breá*)

THE ASPECT OF MADRID, IN THESE DAYS BEFORE the great attack against it began, was considerably less revolutionary than Barcelona, as I was able to see for myself during the following days. The people looked better dressed, and it was less the workers who seemed to dominate the scene of action than the petty bourgeoisie. But the stern and wonderful defence which the city has since put up testified to the strength of its spirit, and it would seem scarcely gallant after such deeds to make too harsh a criticism.

I was struck by the fewer number of buildings on which the red flag flowered, and the way the F.A.I. as a great mass force had dwindled away on the road between Madrid and Catalonia. Fewer places seemed to have been taken over by the workers, less done to break an accepted order. The feeling of war was in the air, in spite of the full cafés, and in the dim city at night the sky seemed empty without the familiar rosy glow which is the nocturnal breathing of great towns.

Between Barcelona and Madrid, there are 400 miles and a revolution. I am not going to insist here on the dialectic whys and wherefores of this distance. I simply note it with some sadness. I reached Barcelona and came to Madrid after July 19th, and had to cross more than one country to get to the revolution under way. On reaching Barcelona, I had the satisfaction of noting that my hasty journey had its "raison d'être," as by arriving in a little later I might have come to Catalonia after the revolution.

Barcelona was a town with all its inhabitants in militia uniform and shirt sleeves, and Catalonia a trades-union population who, from the Ramblas to the heights of Monte Aragon, spoke and thought of nothing but the Socialist revolution, and when referring to the "bourgeois epoch" talked as though it were as far away as the Roman era. In those early times, before the dissolution of the Anti-Fascist Militia Committees, especially, the Catalans were not correcting their errors merely by chance, and were daily advancing in the revolutionary perspective. They had consolidated their objectives with the Council of War, the Economic Council, the Council of Defence, and the Popular Law-Courts.

You may have been led to think that Madrid was the same dog in a different collar, but the contrary is the truth. It was the same collar on a different dog. The anti-Fascist collar was the same as throughout all Spain, but in this case the dog had changed.

Madrid was still the democratic workers' republic of Ortega y Gasset and Co., a republic at war defending the soil of the fatherland to the mixed strains of Riego's hymn and the "Internationale" and as many others as wished to join the choir on condition that none of them got out of tune with the republican concert.

I never understood better how it must have felt to be in Paris when the Germans were on the Marne than when I was in Madrid with the Fascists in the Guadarrama. There is to-day as there was then, a watchword to stand by, and which in these last times has indeed been stood by as much as ever it was during the great war. That watchword is:—"They shall not pass."

The gesture of the people of Paris marked a page of history with one of the most glorious acts known to patriotism. The attitude of the people of Madrid has written in the new history of the world proletariat an epic revolutionary act. The people of Madrid have done everything that could be done, and still more, against Fascism. They shall not pass, and they shall not. But that is not sufficient by itself.

Obviously, at the present time, military heroism is an article of primary necessity for the victory of the revolution. In this respect, we cannot pile up enough splendid adjectives in praise of what has been done at the Madrid fronts.

But what about behind the lines? With the exception of the Spanish Workers' Party, and the Anarchists, both much smaller in Madrid than in Barcelona, all the parties in Madrid are in the war but not in the revolution. The revolution should be unfurled behind the lines while the war is going on at the front, because without a revolutionary rearguard it will be difficult to win the war and impossible to make the revolution. There are no social revolutions without civil wars, but there have always been civil wars without social revolutions. It is therefore useless to confuse the civil war with the revolution. Civil war is only a preparatory step, a more immediate stage towards the revolution. It is not yet by any means the proletarian revolution itself. The first thing which it is vital to do is to identify the civil war with the revolution—it is not sufficient to confuse them—and the only way of doing this by going beyond the objectives of the civil war struggle and transforming them completely into our own objectives. Then, and only then, will we be in condition to win or to lose the war, to win or to lose the revolution, since in any other situation the best which could be hoped would be to win the war while the revolution would always be lost.

It would be idle and unjust to deny that Madrid has passed through a moment of great revolutionary tension. But at the same time one must admit that the revolutionary cycle

has never here, as in Barcelona, developed
sufficiently to rise to the height of the circumstances. The Madrid Government remains
entrenched within the limits of the capitalist
democratic republic and presents the struggle
against Fascism as an end in itself. This is not
in accordance with the aims of the world proletariat, whose interest it is to carry the revolution through to its utmost consequences.

I noted all this almost at once in Madrid,
where the contrast struck me sharply. I was
there for some time, the cold was setting in and
the nearest front was still forty miles away.
Even so, it was a new and singular emotion to
us of Barcelona to be able to take a car and
drive out to the front and back again in the
space of an afternoon.

Cars were put freely at the disposal of journalists by the town of Madrid, and Clara and
some of us determined to go to Toledo. In those
days it still belonged to us and we set out with
Clara's silent, burnt husband and a pair of
militia-men for the guard.

The whole landscape as far as Toledo was a
plain, without even the swelling of a young hill,
and as we drove along our hearts were pinched
by the realisation of how difficult and painful
it would be to defend such country. We talked
about it anxiously most of the way there, aware
of the pressure being made by the enemy in
the Toledo sector. The sky was a hard bright
blue, like enamel, hung above the dried-up

countryside, with the sun like a tambourine in this country where it never goes in, even during the rain.

We saw the city suddenly, rising on slow, gentle hills out of the plain. It seemed rosy, as though it glowed. We passed through a gate to which still hung vestiges of the fortification walls, where two or three militia guards were stationed with their rifles. They all asked us the same questions, and wanted to see the same papers, and gave us finally the same piece of advice:

"You'll need an authorisation from the People's Committee before you'll be able to get out again."

The town rises, going up along the banks of the Tajo which is going down. After passing through the gate, the road goes on and up and becomes a street which ends by being broken off on a barricade which has been flung across it. It was midday. The whole colour of the city of Toledo was ripe and soft.

Whether Tubal, or Hercules built it, or whether it began as Greek Ptolietron, or Jewish Tolededtk neither the Encyclopædia nor Bædeker seem to know, and its historic myth matters little now besides the brief and brilliant rôle it took for a moment as anti-Fascist and proletarian Toledo. It was lifted for a space out of the hands of private property into the first chapters of the history of classless society.

When I saw Toledo, the first legendary stone

of Spanish heraldry, it was as a city clean of
priests and professional soldiers, under the new
emblems of the sickle and the hammer. For
once it was not a centre of international tourism,
and that, perhaps, was what surprised me most
of all in its new aspect. Although this is not
the first time in the history of the city that the
clergy have been put to death and the convents
set on fire, the churches have never before been
used to house committees of the trades union
militias, and this is symptomatic.

In Toledo, when I visited it, as throughout
the rest of anti-Fascist Spain, all the churches
which had not been burned had become vast
public dining-rooms, hospitals, houses for the
people, etc. It was not unusual to see a big
table carted in and placed in front of the high
altar and draped with black and scarlet banners,
and here the People's Committee sat and issued
safe-conducts and passes. In many churches,
images of the saints had still been left intact
and stood there looking down from their niches
with grotesque expressions of divine annoyance
at the revolutionary scene below them. They
must have expected it so little.

We had set out at once to find the People's
Committee to have our passes put in order.
We had begun going through the town in the
car which had brought us, but after trying one
or two streets, in each of which we found ourselves nose to nose with another car with no
way of passing each other in the narrow road,

and had to back out again, we finally decided to go on foot. In the streets, people were sitting in groups chatting at the entrances to houses, and at the passage of a car they got up and lifted their chairs momentarily out of the way without interrupting the conversation. The noise of the cannon and the shooting punctuated all the talk but did not disturb it.

I had not expected to be so near to the firing in Toledo, and was surprised and a little alarmed. The women and children, walking about the streets as though nothing was happening, wore such quiet, tranquil faces and looked so undisturbed that I could not determine which was more real, their faces or the firing. A sudden cannon-shot, nearer and louder than all the rest, made me jump, and a very small child, who had not stopped following me with his eyes ever since we entered the street, dragged at my trouser-leg and assured me that I had nothing to fear because it was our cannon which had made that noise.

We went to see the convent of Santa Cruz. In a Descent from the Cross there a Fascist bullet had gone through Christ's bottom. I thought, what a state the Fascist clergy would be in if they knew how immodestly they had taken aim to have been able to hit the Lord in such a human part of His person. What a lot of paternosters and credos they would be willing to say, and how much penitence to do if only they could take

back that profane shot. I suppose by this time
they have seen what they did and have fully
had time to repent.

"E mando facer (Alfonso VI) un Alcazar,
el cual es hoy alli," though I doubt whether
we could say as much to-day. From the Plaza
de Zocodover, looking towards what was once
the Alcazar, there is nothing recognisable except
a pile of ruins and half a tower standing up like
a broken tooth. All that is left of so much legend
is the famous hill, the seventh hill of Toledo,
like one of the seven hills of Rome to which it
has so often been compared. The Alcazar
to-day has no resemblance left with the Toledan
Military Academy, and when I saw it our flags
were fluttering where the towers once had been
and our soldiers stood where the building used
to stand. A militia-man explained to Clara and
me that the last stone promontory which we
could still see upright was ours on top and Fascist
underneath. There was a deep cellar and a
heavy wall, and it was this wall which remained
between us and the Fascists. However, it was
not so thick but that they had been able to
pierce it here and there from the inside, sufficient
for the protruding nose of a gun or two with
which to take careful aim.

"Isn't there any way of getting at the cellars?"
I asked.

"You can only go in one by one, and it
would be more prudent to be preceded by a
little dynamite."

"Well, I suppose that kind of thing can't be helped," I said with regret and a shrug.

"I'm sorry, for the sake of the women and children," the militia-man said to me. "I've got mine in Badajoz. They shot my father and my brother for refusing to fight on their side. My brother was a fine, intelligent chap, too. My sister got off, because her husband is in the Civil Guard, but the dirty dog won't let her wear mourning."

"Well," he said to me again, after a thoughtful pause, "What else can we do? It's war, you know, and all's fair in that, like in love, isn't it? So you see . . ." and our conversation ended on this discreet allusion to dynamite.

When we had driven down the slope from the town and come a few miles away from it, we came round a curve in the Tajo to see three 15½ cannon in a nest near its bank. We got down from the car because Clara's husband wanted to take some photographs for a Swiss newspaper.

There were some eight or ten men on guard at the cannon emplacement. When the heavy-browed man took his camera out of the canvas sack on his back they drew back.

"Would you mind?" he asked. "I only want to take your picture for some news-papers."

One of them, with a long olive face, put back his head haughtily.

"We don't have our photographs taken," he

said. He added, as though that should have explained everything: "We're Anarchists."

I remembered suddenly that the more conscientious always refused to pose for a picture. It seemed to insult their high revolutionary dignity. I imparted this to Clara's husband, but in his dogged, few worded way he continued to try for a snap.

In the end one of the men came forward and let himself be photographed. Afterwards I learned that he was a Stalinist. He shrugged his shoulders at the remarks made by the others. "Why not?" he asked, truculently justifying his complacency. "Isn't propaganda a weapon, too, just the same as a cannon?"

I couldn't resist firing off a cannon while we were there. It looked so pleasant and easy and was so near at hand. Just a little string to pull. I pulled the little string and was deaf for two days afterwards.

L

XIII

ANOTHER FRONT: SIGUËNZA

(*Narrative by Juan Breá*)

OF ALL THE FRONTS ROUND MADRID, SIGUËNZA,
at the time when I was there, was the farthest
away. It was about 100 kilometres off, past
Alcala de Nares and Guadalajara. I drove out
there in a car with some militia-men, and we
passed great mountains and the deep clefts of
valleys and water cataracting over lips of rock
in a massive, savage landscape. The trees
hung over the road like double rows of parasols.
We had left Madrid in the heat, for the long
Spanish summer was only ending, and now on
the high backs of the mountains we rode at a
temperature of two or three degrees below
zero (centigrade).

The road went up and up, holding close to
the skirts of the mountains while edging along
a precipice, disappearing for a while into the
shadow of the greenery, until at last it reached
the top of the range and rushed down from
there like a whistle towards Siguënza.

Siguënza has about eight or nine thousand
inhabitants, and when we reached it there

were shell holes in the cathedral and the troops belonging to the Spanish Workers' Party were camped in the station. As all the horses in the motor had not yet fallen by the wayside during the steep journey, we drove to the Bishop's Monastery which served as general headquarters

It is a huge block of masonry. The $15\frac{1}{2}$ cannon worry it like terriers pulling at a bull.

Captain Gracia received us.

"If this sort of thing keeps up," he said, showing us the marks on the wall, "repainting the place will cost us a fortune."

"It's all right like that for the time being," interposed a militia-man. "There's no fear of the cold following the cannon balls into the building."

I soon discovered that the cold, in Siguënza, is a theme of an even more absorbing interest than the Carlists themselves. Whatever the Bishop may have done, our lads forgave him freely for having put in central heating.

"Where does the firing line begin?" I asked.

"It begins right here," a man from the C.N.T. militias told me. "You haven't been able to notice it yet because it's Sunday. All the Carlists go to mass on Sundays, and to confession, and as the wretches have any number of crimes to confess to the priest it takes them a long time before they can turn their attention to fighting again. However, when they get through, their artillery starts up near the railway station, about three miles away."

"Is that the nearest advance post?"

"Neither the nearest nor the furthest away. We have one about three-quarters of a mile off, and the furthest one is twenty miles away. We've got them round us like neighbours on all sides here. However, the trains come and go according to schedule in spite of everything, and in spite of the fact that according to the radio the Fascists have captured the line. You can see for yourself that it is free."

In a conversation I had with another militia-man he said to me:

"You know, there's only one thing we're afraid of here. We don't want the war to end before the winter sets in, so that we'd have to go back to Madrid."

"Do you like it here so much, then?"

"Oh," he said, "I'd always dreamed of spending a winter in Siguënza. But how could I? Siguënza has always been a wintering place for rich people, and anyway, whenever winter came round I was always either at work, so that I couldn't go, or else I had no money. But now it looks as though my wish might come true at last, and when the cold weather sets in a little more and we have the first snowfall, I'm going to get hold of a pair of skis."

I began to laugh.

He was indignant.

"Well, why not? If the Carlists have got time to go to mass and confess in wartime, why can't I have time to go ski-ing?"

The Spanish Workers' Party, and the Anarchist Railwaymen's Union, who shared the station and its surroundings for their troops. had requisitioned the houses opposite the railway station in which to billet their men. Our "Lenin" column in Siguënza, like the Spanish Workers' Party itself in Madrid, was a young people's organisation, so young that they had not been able to form a youth section. However, they had a political preparation and a military discipline which any old hand might have envied. The party in Madrid was smaller, of course, but infinitely more revolutionary in every way than in Barcelona. Here it had been formed almost entirely of the old Communist Opposition, while in Catalonia the majority had come from the Workers' and Peasants' Block, which had always been a centrist organisation.

The members of the "Lenin" column, when I met them, were thoroughly at home. They seemed as though they had lived in Siguënza all their lives. Their knowledge of the place, in particular, surprised me. Everyone of them knew the lay of the land as far as two or three kilometres beyond the firing line, and the head man of each group of one hundred men had a little map of the surrounding countryside, and day by day marked on it some new hill or hollow which it might be a good thing to occupy or not.

They used to discuss all this with one of the peasant comrades belonging to the place. He was the one who possessed all the practical knowledge which they needed. They used to ask his opinion, and encourage him to give it because these peasant boys whom they consulted often refused to weigh their word in either way, and as I heard one of them say:

"I won't say yes, and I won't say no. If you like, though, I'll take you over there. But I don't want to have any responsibilities."

"Look here, comrade, this isn't a matter of taking Saragossa, you know. It's only a matter of getting as far as that hill which you've gone up and down so many times in your life. You know it better than we do, and you're the best man to say which is the right place to defend it from, and where to attack."

"But I don't want to take on any responsibilities."

"But if we take your advice, even supposing we fail, it's not your responsibility. It's the Committee's. We don't have to accept your opinion without talking it over, even though, of course, you know more about this than we do. You must get used to thinking of yourself as a comrade just the same as all the rest of us, and you've got the right to use your head now. You don't only have to do as you're told. Take, for example, this business of the hill. In this, you're the one who's got to put forward a plan, then, afterwards, we'll all discuss it together."

A faint bewilderment, then interest, and even a hint of pride moved in the dark, closed face of the peasant.

The comrade who had talked to him struck the iron while it was hot.

"How do you know you mightn't make a good general? Have you ever tried being one?"

At this time, when I was at the Madrid front, things were very different from what they were to be later during the big attack on the city. In those days it all seemed much milder than on the Aragon front. In spite of the systematic visits paid to us by the Fascist aeroplanes and their 100 kilo bombs the war was a guerilla warfare at Siguënza, very different from the Great War flavour of our activities in the north.

Topographically, it was impossible to advance any further than Siguënza. There we had pushed the front out in a wedge, and the enemy were on three sides of us. On one side the firing line was twenty miles away—we had had to go that far to make contact with the enemy—and on another it was impossible to judge how far off one was. There were villages in between which had not been taken by either us or them. Sometimes we used to send out about fifty comrades to go and fetch provisions from one of these villages. They used to go and come back laden. The next day the Fascists would go and take what was left.

I decided to go with some men in a car to the furthest advance post. When we came to a certain point, we had to leave the car by the side of the road and walk up the mountain side for the last five or six kilometres.

Presently we came to a sentinel.

"How do we get to the last outpost?" we asked.

"Up there, on the crest of that hill. But you'd better take care and go slow. We had a smatter of fire just now, and the chaps who ought to take over haven't come back. Of course, they may be at the house taking a cup of coffee. . . ."

"We'll go carefully all right."

"You'd better. Before you get there it's safer to give Julio a call. Yell out, 'Reds.' If you hear him answer, 'Against Fascism,' then you can go on safely."

We went on, dodging very carefully. It felt like a film. The landscape was silent and seemed full of secrets.

"Reds!"

There was a pause. Then a voice came back with a deep echo:

"Against Fascism."

We went up.

Fortunately, nothing had happened. The militia guard who were to take over came back intact and satisfied after their hot coffee at "Aunt Juana's."

"Take a picture of us for the papers?" one of them suggested to me. I had a camera slung on my back.

"Right-oh."

I got the thing out of its case and began fixing the focus.

"What do you want your picture taken for?"

another man asked indignantly. "Do you think you're going to come out in the papers on account of your pretty face, or what?"

"Well, Pepe came out."

"I know. But Pepe captured a machine-gun from the Fascists."

"Is it my fault that the five Fascists that we got last Sunday hadn't a machine-gun with them?"

Another militia-man said to me:

"Did you see those three chaps who came over from the other side and joined our ranks last week? One of them is a boy from my village. He's called Casimir. Suppose you took a picture of him? No one will say that he doesn't deserve it."

"I have taken a photograph of him," I said.

I had. It came out in the Barcelona papers, too, with three boys kneeling in the sun, the photo all hard black and white angles, and the boys with their bare arms up and fists clenched and saluting, and all of them smiling. Casimir was at the end of the row. It was the last photograph he was to have taken. A few days later he fell under the Fascist bullets, young and fighting bravely.

I thought of a conversation I had had with him.

He had been telling me about some prisoners that had been taken by the Fascists while he was still serving in their army and looking for a way of escape.

"They were three men, and a woman," he said. "They didn't tell us what they were going to do with them. They often kept dark about what happened to workers they took prisoner, and especially as there was a woman this time, the officers had it spread round that they were to be sent back to their own villages."

"Did they ever do that?"

He shook his head.

"I don't know. I don't think so, their attitude was always brutal. But I know what happened to those prisoners, because I had to wait on the officers that day at their lunch and they talked in front of me.

"'Well, have you had those four prisoners shot yet?' one of the officers inquired.

"'Yes, dead and done for, the four of them this morning,' the captain answered.

"You should have heard the casual way they talked about it, as though it had been so many heads of cattle. And the doctor guffawed, and winked at the captain.

"'Four? You mean the five prisoners, surely?'

"'I thought there were four. . . . Three men and a woman, weren't there?'

"The doctor winked again, and seemed to be enjoying a great joke.

"'No, five, my dear sir. Ah, the woman, you forget that the woman was . . . well . . .'

"You know," Casimir had said bitterly to me, "they all laughed like anything over that. They really thought the doctor was a great one!"

When I had taken some photographs, we went back again to the town. We used to be served lunch in the open air, sitting about in the fields near the station. We were with some of the Anarchists as well as our own men. That day we had the Political Commissar with us when we went to eat.

We were talking, our tin plates held on our knees, when a militia-man came over with a bottle with a long slender spout and offered it to us for a drink.

We took it each in turn, and put our heads back, and the stream of water leaped out and curved in an arc into our mouths. The militia-man sat down on the ground cross-legged and began to tell us about the taking of Siguënza.

He had a round head, like a nut, and the black hair grew down almost to the arches of his brows. When he grew animated, as he talked, a sudden blue flame darted out of his luminous eyes. The commissar looked at him with a curious smile.

"Oh yes, it was very tough," he said, endorsing the boy. "The Civil Guard was defending it, and of course their military training and all the rest of it stood them in good stead."

"Oh, the Civil Guard," the boy cried out, in his hoarse, guttural voice, and at the same time the eyes gleamed and sparkled again with that too clear light under the ribbon of brow.

"I know them well, I can tell you. Have a look!"

He bent towards us, and pulled open the zip fastener of his militia shirt. He showed us a scarred place on his back.

"I got that when they were beating me. It was about two years ago." It was a long, rambling story, and he told it, darting his bright look at us from time to time. "But still," he said, rocking himself with pleasure and a delight like a child's, "I was able to take my revenge quite all right, all right. You should have seen. A lot of them saw. It was when we were taking Sigüenza, after all that that I told you already, and then some of the Civil Guards that had been wounded went and took refuge in the cathedral. When we got in there after them, there was a big fat sergeant lying there on the floor, and when he saw me he looks up and says:

"'Water! Water!'

"There wasn't much stuffing in him then. It's not like when they're taking a lick at you. So I says:

"'Certainly. Here you are.'

"And there was a water jug like this one"— he touched the one from which we had drunk— "and I picked it up and took it to him, and him lying there with his eyes shut and his mouth open waiting for me to put the spout in. So I says:

"'Here you are.'

"And I shoved the nose of my revolver in his mouth and pulled the trigger.

"You should have seen how he looked afterwards."

He hugged himself happily, and gave us a blazing look, and the first roots of his hair seemed to touch his nose.

When he got up and went away the commissar shrugged and fetched a deep sigh.

"What can one do?" he said. "Those are the sort of people we have to shoot when the revolution is over."

We were still lunching when a woman in militia costume with dark hair like pulled silk flying round her face came and joined us. She had a revolver stuck in her belt, and came up with four militia-men.

They were in a state of great excitement, and all burst out talking at once as soon as they reached us. They were all trying to tell the same tale, piling one version on top of the other. They had been out for a reconnoitre trip, and had seen a house, and were getting quite near to it, when suddenly all the doors and windows began to spit bullets at them. They'd only got away with their skins in the nick of time.

"Who is she?" I asked.

"She's the wife of our captain, Etchebehere," the commissar answered. He spoke with deep affectionate respect. His tone of voice, and the present tense which he still used, showed me a thousand times better than all the praise he

might have sung how dear Hipolito Etchebehere
must have been to this heroic woman, and that
for her at least he was not yet dead.

"I've wanted to meet you very much, comrade," I said, thinking of all I had heard about
her and Etchebehere.

We talked. She spoke French and German
to a Swiss who was there, talking in a soft,
fluent voice with little movements of her
wrists and hands, half affectation and half
natural. I learned then from her that she was
Argentine, a doctor, and a Trotskyist—though
I should have guessed the latter.

When I said something about getting safely
through the war, she threw back her head and
hair and said:

"Oh, don't wish that mischance on me."

She had been working in an ambulance ever
since the beginning of the war, and her husband
had been in command of our troops in the
Sigüenza sector. All the wounded had passed
through her hands for first aid. Only one had
not passed through them, one she had not been
able to cure. She was never to see him again,
neither dead nor wounded. It was the fine edge
of irony that it should have been her own
husband.

When he died, she had handed the bandages
to someone else and taken up a gun to fill his
empty place.

I imagine well how she must have stood guard
in the long, cold watches of the night, out at

the Atienza advance post, in a stillness like a South American nocturne, always watching a little mound on the face of the hill and hoping to see a shadow come back from there where he fell not to rise again.

I left Siguënza and went back to Madrid. Two days later, the Fascist attack on Siguënza broke out from all sides, and our troops were driven back again from the little wedge they had conquered beyond the general outline of the front. The last stronghold in which our militias held out was the cathedral. Some got away at last, others were massacred there.

A long time after this, Mary and I saw Mica Etchebehere in Barcelona, in an old pair of plus fours and a militia shirt.

"I was there till the last," she said. We sat in three high, striped chairs in the hall of a pension. She still moved her hands like birds. "We barricaded ourselves in the cathedral— those of us who had been trapped in the town— and determined to put up a good show for our money. We were there for four days, without food or anything, firing out into the town, and dying like flies. They kept on shooting cannon balls into the cathedral. It stood up to it pretty well, but in the end the walls began to fall down on us, and we had no ammunition left at all, so those of us who were still left decided to make a run for it after dark as we couldn't fight any more."

"It must have been awful."

"It was awful. There was a thick fog on the night we made the get-away, and some of the comrades got lost and ran straight into the Fascists and were shot to pieces. They began firing on us at once, of course, and we scattered and reached the woods through a rain of machine-gun bullets. I wandered about for twenty-four hours, hiding among the trees and undergrowth, while they hunted me, before I could reach our lines. They shot lots of us, of course. About a third of us who set out from the cathedral reached home. I was almost delirious from exhaustion and want of food."

I felt full of my admiration for her. She sat there in the chair, leaning back tiredly, the ends of the plus fours unstrapped and dangling down to her brogues, no longer a very young woman.

"I wonder why I always escape?" she said, making one of her affected gestures. "Why does it have to be me?"

"Life's very tenacious, in spite of everything," I said.

"In spite of myself, above all."

She smiled, her dark, dead eyes looking out below the aureole of hair.

"But I'm going back," she said. "I'm going back to the Madrid front. I'm heading a brigade of special shock troops to look after the most dangerous sectors."

Some time later, Mary was able to print the following notice:

"Our Militias at the Madrid Front:

"Our shock troops operating in the Moncloa sector at the Madrid front, under Comrade Mica Etchebehere, have greatly distinguished themselves for their valour in action. Yesterday they took several tanks from the enemy."

A few weeks later she was dead.

M

XIV

WOMEN . . .

(*Narrative by Mary Low*)

WE WERE BACK ONCE MORE IN BARCELONA. WE
were busy. I was working at a newspaper to
sell in England, and Breá was giving lectures on
dialectics and historic materialism.

Things had changed in Barcelona. The war
was here now as much as the revolution, and
possibly more than the revolution. There were
more foreigners about, and everything was better
organised and went quicker. The International
Column was not the same. Numbers of the
original members lay wounded or were dead,
and other young men had come out from different countries to take their place. Many bled
to death at outposts along the Aragon front for
lack of medical supplies and ambulances. By
this time it had ceased to seem strange or shock-
ing, as when they had carried Robert back, and
become the usual routine of nightmare. We
settled down.

About this time, anti-Fascist countries who
could not make up their minds to send men were
sending money and medical aid at last. Nurses

and ambulances came from England. Many
actually did go to the front, but some had a
royal time in Barcelona, living in private villas
that were lent to them free of charge and
being gushed over by female reporters. Some
of the men attached to them were so drunk
about the streets that they had to be sent home.
All this was done with money given by the
English workers in their poverty.

There were other sorts of ambulance people.
There was fat Eva, who went out with the
"Joaquim Maurin" car sent by the I.L.P. She
was a stolid young German girl, who took the
ambulance almost up to Huesca during a big
attack. Martin, the Irish artillery commander,
found her alone in the dressing-station, her hands
red to the wrists.

"It isn't anything," she said with her fat
smile, her straw hair a little untidy. "Anyone
could do it."

The bullets were pinging like tennis balls.

I tried hard to persuade Margaret Zimbal
("Putz") to go to the front with an ambulance
instead of with the militias, she seemed so
needlessly young and fair for death. But she
laughed, sitting astride a chair in corduroy
overalls with a red handkerchief slung round
her neck.

"Well, what do you think about it?" I asked,
when I had exhausted myself in argument.

She laughed and tweaked my nose.

"I think you talk a lot," she said.

I remember seeing her for the first time. It was a long time ago, the night the men came back after failing to take Majorca. It was the first failure, and I remember the local as very quiet, people hanging about mournfully and whispering. Putz had lost her lover, a young German boy who had been massacred in Porto Cristo. She came up the stairs slowly, with more than the weight of the gun bowing her back.

We stood round her, while she told us in brief Spanish, with a high singing accent, of the taking of Porto Cristo. How they had left too few men there to guard it while they took the ships round to attack from the other side. How the Fascists had swooped down and massacred the defenders.

"Yes," she said, "he's dead." She crammed back some hair that had escaped out of her bun. "Well, I shall go to another front as soon as possible, that's all."

There was no room immediately in the local for all the men who had come back from Majorca. People slept on mattresses strewn all over the floor. In the morning I went to the room where she had slept with some other girls.

She was lying on the floor, gloriously young and naked, with her yellow hair streaming in folds over the pillow. She showed me a little sketch book where she had noted all her impressions of two years tramping through Spain with her boy.

"He used to play the guitar," she said, "and we sang. We had no other way of living. We ran away from home because our parents were Fascist and wanted us to be, too. We slept out under the trees. It was fun."

She was burnt brown.

In the book there were some pictures of fat Germans she had come across, wintering abroad, with pimples on their faces and thick necks. Underneath them she had scrawled: "Four times Aryan." Sometimes they had spoken to her, and been very shocked that Germans should be singing in the street. One woman offered to pay her fare back to Germany, through the consulate, if only she would go home and be a good girl.

Putz was nineteen. Her father was a professor at Dusseldorf University. She looked at the lady with simple sweetness, and said:

"I'm a Jew."

The woman gave her ten centimes and went hastily away.

Two days after the return from Majorca, Putz left for the Aragon front with four young Spanish boys. They all had packs on their backs and went away singing. They had only been at the front six hours when the boys were shot down in couples on either side of her, and she was left alone. Afterwards she wrote to us sometimes from the mountains, where she was acting as scout, creeping at night over the dark hills on the borders of no-man's land, not knowing how far from the enemy's advance posts she might be. Then she was back in Barcelona again, doing political work and attending the International Bureau.

We thought we had her then. She was under the thumb of a thick German man, with a squashed nose and hairy hands, who had done great deeds at the front. She was not one to be long without a man. Yet she resented him after the dead boy, arguing, chaffing, running off and leaving him alone in the café and shrugging her wide, fine shoulders. He wouldn't let her go back to the militia. She wore black corduroy suits, and an old beret, and her face looked smooth and serene, as though nothing had happened to her, as though she had come from school. She was clever and worked hard.

One day we were there in the café with her, when her old company, the "Bandera Puig" had been called back to the front. We could hear the trumpets blowing. Putz was swinging on her chair, sucking a straw, and her quiet face was inscrutable. We saw them come marching down the street, the dust rising and the red flag fluttering. They passed us.

Suddenly Putz jumped up and threw away her chair and ran after them all down the street, crying, "Wait for me, wait for me, I'm coming too! I'm coming."

We never saw her alive again. She was outside Huesca, bending down over a militia-man who had fallen and feeling his heart, when

a sharp-shooter got her. The ball went through
her back and she fell down instantly.

The thick German brought her back in a
lorry to Barcelona. They laid her in state in a
theatre which belonged to the party, all the
walls hung with glowing red, and the sickle and
hammer starting out huge and white and
triumphant from floor to ceiling. There were
wreaths of red flowers on the floor, and hour after
hour people shuffled by with their militia caps
dangling from their hands. We, in our best
stiff blue uniforms for town parade, formed a
woman's guard of honour, standing rigid in
relays for twenty-four hours. She had a veil
flung over her, pink in the red glow. She looked
very well, her head a little oddly held, but not
changed at all.

Everyone sent delegations to the funeral, and
used it as a political platform for women's
manifestos.

Times were hard for the Germans and Italians
in Barcelona, as they had lost their nationality
for taking part against the Fascists. The remedy
against this was easier for the women than for
the men.

I remember sitting in a café at night, after
work was over temporarily, with Breá, and
Calero, the barrister-second-in-command of the
International Column. He was now back on
leave from the Alcubierre mountains, very thin
and gay. Serna, the lame lawyer and district
judge, was there too. Unfortunately he became

more Anarchist every day. He was an old friend, very good and kind. We were with a German girl, Lili, who worked for the radio, in despair because her passport had been annulled.

I remember we were talking about the new marriage laws and the status of women under the revolution. I wanted an article for our English paper.

"Look here, Serna," I said, "you're a judge and know it all. Can't you do me an article on the New Marriage and Divorce?"

"I'll try," he said. "Anyway, I could let you have all the details, and the statistics."

"I wish you would. I read daily in the foreign Press the glorified numbers of the divorces we have had so far in Catalonia. But nothing about the marriages, which seem to me at least equally important."

"Heaps more," Calero said. "Most of the men appointed to the new law courts are old friends of mine, and I can tell you all about it. People are marrying like flies in summer. It's quite easy, you can marry whoever you like without giving notice, and it only takes five minutes all told. No formality."

He showed us a marriage certificate form.

When I read it I was very delighted that our Andres Nin was Minister of Justice and had done it all. There was a paragraph in it addressed to the husband which said:

"You are asked to remember that your wife

goes into marriage as your companion, with the same rights and privileges as yourself."

It added that women were equal to men, that the revolution had restored them to their natural place in society and could admit of no sex domination.

Calero was pleased at my pleasure, rubbing his dry, crackly hands together and chuckling. "That's what we do," he said. "That's what they ought to tell in the foreign papers."

He was a bachelor. I asked Serna:

"What do you think of that?"

"I think it's fine. Especially here. Women were barbarously treated before."

"Well, why do you leave your own wife shut up just as you did before? I never see her out with you."

He was furiously indignant, and stamped his walking stick on the ground, his black eyes snapping.

"What on earth do you mean? Of course she comes out with me. It's not at all the same as before. Why, I take her to the cinema at least twice a week!"

I realised then how hard the old mould was to crack in spite of the best good will. I began to laugh.

Lili was worrying, trying to get the two boys who knew all the revolutionary law-courts to do something about her status.

"I think you should marry someone," Calero decided at last, after mature deliberation. "Of course, it's a little difficult if you have no papers, but I think I could fix it for you. Yes, you must get married, preferably to a Frenchman— or even a Spaniard would do quite well."

Lili turned her eyes towards her companion, Louis.

"Of course," Louis said, thoughtfully, "and we would be able to travel in France, then, and everything. Why not, dear? If we can find someone to consent to a blank marriage."

Calero was singing to himself, gay and nonchalant. He was tapping the edge of the table with his fingers. His mellow voice was throbbing in the room.

He looked up quietly.

"Why not?" he asked. "Do you think any revolutionary could refuse, when you know how little importance we attach to formulas of that kind?" He flung out his hand, with one of the grand, careless gestures learned in the South, and said, "Marry me, if you like," and went on singing.

"Oh, Calero. That's good of you. But are you sure you wouldn't mind?"

"What for? Besides, anything for a friend like Louis."

A little later I went to the law-courts with a Spanish friend and the Frenchwoman with whom he had lived for ten years.

"We've decided to get married," he'd told me. "It's silly, of course, and unnecessary, and counter-revolutionary, and all that, but I want her to have the nationality. It'll be easier for her here, and she'll be better looked after while I'm at the front."

Her name was Simone, and her birth certificate and the papers they needed were in Dieppe and could not be got hold of. The men in session at the courts did not seem to mind, and waived it all with charming courtesy and good humour.

"Name? . . . Name of mother? . . . Name of father . . . ?"

"I never had a father."

She said it painfully, and blushed.

They smiled at once, kind and encouraging. They treated it as a fine idea. One of them slapped her new husband on the back.

"Good for you," they said.

To them it really seemed quite right and sensible.

They asked for the witnesses, and then found that one of them had not brought his identity papers.

"I'll go back and get them. I forgot. I won't be long."

"It doesn't matter. Don't go, I think I know your father. Didn't he live at 29, Rierez Alta?"

"Yes."

"Then it's all right. I know who you are and we'll take you on trust. Come along, sign here. Have a cigarette?"

They shook hands, laughed. It was over and had taken five minutes.

"And the divorce?" I asked.

"That only takes five minutes, too, and it's quite easy."

"What grounds do you admit?"

"Oh, the wife has all the same permitted reasons for divorcing her husband as he had for divorcing her. Besides that, if two people come to us and want to divorce and seem determined about it, we don't see any reason for muddling their lives for them. We don't prevent them from having a fresh start."

It seemed to me clean and reasonable.

"Either of the parties can marry again. But they have to wait thirty days to make sure that the woman is not with child so that paternity can be acknowledged by the right father."

I said:

"I suppose in time they will come to realise that marriage and divorce are equally senseless in the new society, where women don't need men's protection and have their own status and earning powers."

The Spanish women were anxious to grab their liberty, but they had been closed up and corsetted so long that they didn't know how much of it there was to be had. Often they were content with the little scraps which answered their first call. It seemed so much to them.

The Anarchist trade unions had begun a group, "Free Women," which issued manifestos

and edited a splendid paper. I knew one of
the girls on the editorial committee. She was
deep-bosomed and sweet, and talking to her
you could see that she had realised more
than the average woman what freedom could
mean.

"They're so eager," she explained, "and so
determined to be free. But most of them don't
even know what freedom means. They're
not stupid, only untrained to think, uneducated
except in the art of pleasing. But they are
awfully courageous, and full of determination.
It's wonderful raw material."

She wrote clever things, and organised well.
Later a French revolutionary fell in love with
her, and she loved him, too. But when it came
to bed, she refused with a comic and desperate
virtue.

"Why not? Isn't it natural when one's in
love?" she told me that he asked her. He had
been hurt by her attitude.

"And why wouldn't you?" I asked.

"Oh, because one hasn't time for all that
kind of thing during the revolution."

"It's not true," I said. "It's an excuse. You
only say it to hide your prejudices."

She looked at me, and then shrugged.

"Well, after all, one can't really be expected
to change over night, can one?"

The religious heritage was very hard to get
rid of.

The family was another thing. Louise Gomez,

Gorkin's wife, charming and energetic, decided to build a women's secretariat in the party, and form a women's regiment and women's classes and lectures and centres of education and child welfare. She received more than 500 adherants within the first week (it shows you something of their eagerness), but dozens of full-blown matrons, and young girls confided to me:

"Of course I wasn't able to tell my husband (or my father) that I was coming here, he would have had a fit. I just had to say I was joining a sewing-circle."

The regiment was composed in large part of these runaways. We used to meet at seven o'clock in front of the local, with the winter morning mist still rolling up the Ramblas and round the trunks of the trees, strapped into our new blue wollen uniforms with divided skirts and stand there blowing on our hands and most of us hoping that our families wouldn't catch us.

I have seldom seen such spirits. They were so glad and gay and seemed like children. While we waited for the members of the Directive Committee to come and lead us to the barracks they skipped on the hard pavement and played little girls' games, singing and holding hands and dancing in their pointed shoes. (It was a long time before we could make them all understand that they must go to drill in flat heels and leave their earrings at home.) In the excitement of being free, they were able to get up carelessly

time after time in the rough morning air. They
would wait endlessly on the drill-field in the wind.
Even the weight of centuries of indolence did
not deter them.

We used to go to the barracks, which were a
long way out from the centre of the town. On
the way, in the tram or the metro, the militia-
boys used to chaff us. We sang the "Internationale" very loudly and tried to convince
them that our uniform was as serious as their
own. Sometimes they ended by being impressed.
They would stand whispering gravely together
and looking at us seriously out of their thick-
lashed eyes.

It was a long road from the tram-stop to the
barracks. We swung along it in formation. The
men leaned out of passing lorries and grinned
at us and raised their fists and yelled:

"Comrades!"

"Comrades!" we yelled back in chorus and
raised our fists too.

I remember the first day when we all lined
up to file past the guards at the entrance to
the barracks. How they stared, and afterwards laughed and cheered us, and all the
regiments turned out to see us go by. We felt
proud. A French boy ran down into the
courtyard from one of the galleries, and
demanded crossly:

"Now what do you think you're all doing?"
He looked as though he had a grievance. He
had come back from the front.

"We're coming to learn to fight," I said, with some pride. "We're a battallion."

"Well, it's no use," he said, quickly. "I wouldn't have women at the front at all, if I had the choice. I've been there and I know."

"Why? Don't you think we're capable? Not brave enough?"

"It's not that," he said. "Far from it. There may have been something in that at the first, when crowds of untrained girls went there without knowing what they were going to, and so forth, but that was due to the confusion. Of course, everything had been organised since then. Oh, I haven't a word against the militia-women at the front for their courage, or what they can do, or any of that. Oh, no."

"Then what are you driving at?" Why do you object?"

He gave a little, tired sigh.

"You see," he said, "it makes everything altogether too heroic. Especially for the Spaniards. They're conscious of being males every moment of the day and night, you know I mean. They haven't got rid of their old-fashioned sense of chivalry yet, however silly they may think it is. If one of you girls get caught by the enemy, fifteen men immediately risk their lives to avenge her. All that kind of thing. It costs lives and it's too much effort."

"Then they must get over it," somebody said. "And they never will unless we go on as we're doing."

"In any case," we explained for his greater comfort and joy, "you can rest yourself about this battallion. We don't put it up as a principle that women ought to go to the front, we don't think that, we only want to give a hand to all the individual cases who are good at that sort of thing. As for the rest of us here, we all have our own social or political work to attend to."

"Then why are you drilling?"

"How dense you are," Louise cried, while the early sun glinted on the polished shoes of the horses which were galloping riderless round and round the yard, "because human beings should be properly equipped for defence when they are liable to be attacked. Supposing Barcelona was shelled? It would be silly if we couldn't do anything—a bunch of sheep, like in bourgeois countries."

We went into an underground shooting gallery. It was stone paved, and the echo battered at one's ears, rebounding back endlessly from wall to wall.

The first day we were there the sergeant walked quietly to the back of the gallery while we stood facing the targets and let off a shot behind our backs without warning. Everybody screamed. Louise Gomez came out firmly to the front and said:

"If that ever happens again, that is the end of the Women's Battallion."

It never did happen again.

We drilled for four hours without stopping, in every weather. The officers took us with full

N

seriousness. They would not let the men come into the field and look on, and walked beside the leaders, patiently stamping the earth flat with their boots while giving us the beat. The drummers walked tirelessly in front of us to mark out the time. It was amazing that nobody ever complained, or fell out, or failed to come again. Some of their bodies were stiff and awkward, out of corsets for the first time. Yet they bore it all, and returned for more.

After the shooting and the drilling we used to have machine-gun practice. "Just supposing one of these things fell into your hands and you couldn't work it," as the instructor, with his cap lazily pushed over one eye, used to explain. It was the only thing which was really difficult. We had no mechanical turn, and spent a long time learning to take all the parts of the machine to pieces and put them correctly together again, and besides, the machine was so hard and heavy for us. But we did learn. In the end, I think that we could have assembled the parts of a machine-gun in the dark, without a clank to show the enemy where we were hidden, and fired it off as a surprise.

I remember we were very proud of this, and mentioned it in the next manifesto we issued.

The Women's Secretariat had grown enormous, and every day we requisitioned more rooms to house us all. Hundreds of women came every day to attend classes on socialism, child welfare, French, hygiene, women's rights, the origin of

the religious and family sense, and to knit
and sew and make flags and discuss, and read
books. It was a great success. One had to
begin from the first steps, like with young
children.

Louise Gomez was one of the best of all the
organisers, energetic, and at the same time
gentle and gay. She was big and full, and I
remember her always going to and coming
from something with a warm, contented face
and grey fur on her arms. She was French,
and not the only one. I remember Simone,
too, who was bringing arms and could not get
past the frontier with them, and the pilot of
the aeroplane she took would not land in Spain.
So she jumped out of the aeroplane into Catalonia
with a parachute on her shoulders and machine-
gun-rifles strapped to her body. Afterwards I
talked to a young Catalan kid, with a cropped
head, who had been in the same trench with
her.

"She was game," he said. "She was an
awful wildcat, though." He rubbed the stubble
on his scalp with the palm of a reminiscent hand.
"She got us out of some situations. We hadn't
been under fire before, and when the Fascists
made the first big attack and came right over
at us, Pepe and I really thought that everything
was up with us and we had better run for it.
But not she! She knocked our heads together
—how it hurt—yes, she really had time to
think of everybody in a moment like that—

and pushed us back by the scruff of our necks."

"And did you hold the position?"

"Oh yes," he said, and it seemed to make him tired even to think about the long effort it had been, standing so long with the water up to his knees. "Oh yes, we held it. We kept on holding it, you know."

It was when I had come back from the drill-field one Sunday, covered in mud and water, and was going along the endless corridors to my room, that two men jumped out at me from behind a door and shoved the noses of their revolvers into my back.

"Put 'em up," they said.

I did as I was told. I had a revolver on my hip, but they relieved me of it.

I didn't know either of their faces.

"You wouldn't mind telling me, I suppose——"

"Show us your papers."

"In there," I said, nodding to my right pocket.

They pulled them out and one of them fumbled while the other watched me.

I had everything in order. Women's Regiment papers, free circulation pass in anti-Fascist territory, radio section appointment, journalist card. There was nothing to be said.

They gave me back my revolver and slipped their own into their holsters. One of them slapped me on the shoulders.

"Sorry, comrade. We've been wrong. I hope you won't hold it against us."

"It might happen to anyone," I said. I was breathing easier. I knew I was all right, but it had made me pant. "What's up?" I asked.

"If you knew the game they've been giving us. There are two spies have been detected in the local, one of them a woman, and now, of of course, they know we've spotted them and they're in hiding. We've been——"

At that moment there was a rushing of starched skirts and an elderly figure with grey hair burst past us into my room beyond, brandishing a glittering automatic attached to her waist by a chain.

"You won't mind me looking under your bed, will you? You never now where they'll be hiding."

This latter intervention I judged to be unnecessary and dramatic, but Dolores was like that. She was an old woman, horsey, extraordinarily strong.

"I'm half Scotch," she would tell you, with a strong Spanish accent. "I have about thirty-six members of my family living in Scotland."

All her statements were gaudy, grandly delivered. I went to see her once when she was lying ill in bed, her head swathed in pink cotton-wool. (All the local became completely disordered when she was laid up, for her stiff tongue and frightful language were the only means of keeping the hot Catalan heads in order). She lay there, rolling her eyes about in the gaunt brick-and-white face her nose jutting out and the nostrils pinching.

"Ah, all my old wounds come back to me when I am tired and ill."

She threw a leg out of bed suddenly, with long white sinews and a mark like a cross on the thigh.

"Do you see that? Guess where I got it?"

"I can't imagine." She was too old to have been at these fronts.

"On the Italian front, my girl, during the Great War."

"But you're not Italian?"

"What's the odds?" She rolled her eyes at me and pinched the old wound till it throbbed livid. "I went off with a captain of Bersaglieri. I wore pants and a feather in my cap, I tell you. It was that feather which nearly did for me, too. We were lying out behind a big stone, on the edge of no-man's-land, three of us, and they were potting at us all day and we couldn't move away from the stone. I was never so stiff in all my life. They got both the others, and I lay there between both of them dead until it was dark and I could crawl away. But they had me here in the leg. I wondered why for a long time their shots always came so near. Then I saw that the feather in my cap had been waving all the time. Oh dear, oh dear, what a long time ago."

She fell into a comatose reverie and I crept off.

I think her daughter was religious, though she never said so, and kept the girl out of sight. Anyway, she was living in a house where some clergy were in hiding, and when the clergy were taken and arrested, the girl was shot.

Dolores went to the Morgue to identify her. Afterwards I found her sitting in her glass cage, wrapped in an old wool shawl and her hands under her armpits, doddling her head from side to side.

"No, I'm not sure, I couldn't really identify her," she muttered when I asked her. "Her head had fallen on one side, and the hair all over the face, but I recognised the watch and a ring she used to have. Only she seemed much stouter. They wouldn't let me stand her up to see if she was the right height, either. They wouldn't let me touch her at all. Well, perhaps it's better."

She became less clear after that, if more virulent in roaring after the boys to keep them in order, and sometimes seemed to wander. The last I saw of her, she brandished a stick at me and told me all about a number of spies she had arrested. Then she said:

"This life's too quiet for me. I'm off. If I'm too old to fight I'm going in one of the ambulances." She added aggressively, with her thin bright lips pinched: "I'm a trained nurse, though you mightn't know it."

I was sorry when she went. She had liked me and used to give me fruit and milk "to make you nice and fat " according to Spanish taste.

When I was working with the Women's Secretariat we had been planning numbers of posters. Most of them I thought out of line, and sentimental. They harped a good deal on family feeling. It took a long time shaking people out of their old mould. The Anarchist women were more ambitious as far as posters were concerned. They attacked all kinds of problems with their slogans.

I was riding in the tram down the Ramblas the first time I saw their poster against prostitution. It was the first time I had seen the matter raised. I felt very pleased at this new sight.

The poster was huge and covered a whole hoarding. Everyone was looking at it.

A group of Anarchists from the militias, the young beards fresh on their faces, were standing round me on the rattling front of the tram. When they saw it they were disturbed.

"Finish with prostitution," read one of them. "What do you think of that?"

They stood around uneasily, obviously annoyed, and awkward at finding themselves annoyed.

"Our women, too. They don't mind getting their hand in, do they?"

"Nothing to do with them. They're free, aren't they?"

"Well, what's a man going to do if they

start really suppressing it? It's not as though
they were so oncoming themselves that we could
do without it."

At night the narrow streets in the prostitute
quarter swarmed with militias back from the
front.

"Well, what can you do?" people answered
me with a shrug. "You can stop it growing, or
beginning again, but what can you do with those
women who are there already? How can you
change them?"

"They might go to work in the factories. Or
nurse. Or they might go to the front."

"So they did go to the front at first. But
being hardened by prostitution doesn't necessarily
make one cool under fire. A lot of them were
in the way, and then the men were always
being sent home with venereal because there
was no control."

"I don't care. Something ought to be done
for them."

"The militias would growl, and they deserve
a lot of indulgence for the fight they're putting
up. People don't understand things all in a
rush. You have to be patient sometimes. And
above all, you have to change the mentality of
the women in this country first."

In the end, the prostitutes began to look after
their own interests. A little time had elapsed
before they began thinking of vindicating themselves. One day they realised that they also
could be in the revolution.

Immediately they turned out the patrons to whom the houses belonged and occupied the "working premises." They proclaimed their equality. After a number of stormy debates, they formed a trade-union and presented a petition for affiliation to the C.N.T.

All profits were equally shared. Henceforth, instead of the usual former picture of the "Sacred Heart," a framed notice was hung up in every brothel announcing:

"You are requested to treat the women as comrades.
"The Committee.   (By order.)"

The average woman in the street continued in most respects to look the same as before the revolution—that is to say that superfluous wealth and luxury had disappeared on the backs of the former ruling caste, but the women continued to have high heels and beautiful hair and to follow a dress style which is only ever in vogue in Spain. There was one marked difference, though. The mantillas, with their religious symbolism, had been torn to shreds and now everyone went bareheaded in sun and rain. The Anarchists had made a heavy campaign against hats.

XV

THE COUNCIL OF THE GENERALITY OF CATALONIA

(Narrative by Mary Low)

THE GENERALITY OF CATALONIA WAS HOUSED IN several imposing buildings in different quarters of the town, but its greatest activities were centred in the Aragon Palace. This, and another vast mansion opposite to it, also occupied by the Generality, dominated a little square on top of a hill in the middle of the town. The square was always thick with cars. Guards, dressed in the special government uniform, which was blue, very complicated and covered with silver buttons, stood about everywhere and watched over all the entrances.

"The Ministry of Finance?" I asked. I spoke to an elderly guard, with bad teeth, who stood warming himself like a bird in the November sunshine. His arms were lifted out slightly from the sides of his body like wings, or like the flaps of a penguin.

"First floor, then to the right."

I passed under the archways behind his back into an inner courtyard. A staircase faced me made of marble, the balustrade carved intricately with vine-leaves and the pillars so slim that they seemed brittle. I went up these stairs and then walked through Moorish arches round a central square where orange trees like toys were growing, and a fountain playing. On the other side was a huge hall, dark, its high ceiling covered with gilt. "Finance" stared at me haughtily over one of the doors.

A guard was standing in front of the door. I went by him and seized the handle.

"Pardon me," he said, interposing himself with speed and firmness.

"What's the matter?"

"Stand away, please. You can't go in like that. It's the Ministry of Finance."

"I know. That's what I've come for."

He looked at me coldly. I had a red handkerchief tied round my neck, and was wearing militia uniform.

"You'll have to wait in the ante-room and send in a card stating your business if you want to be seen."

I was furious.

"I didn't come to the revolution to wait about in ante-rooms. Don't you suppose I've had all my life and the rest of Europe to do that in? Let me in."

He looked superior at the word revolution.

"This is the Generality," he said.

So it was, and I had now ample time to realise what that meant. When, much later, I stood in the department of the Ministry of Finance, they did not ask me to be seated but kept me there while they talked for a moment idly among themselves, flipping paper-knives over their polished nails and stifling a sophisticated yawn.

The room was tapestried from floor to ceiling and had thick carpets. The bureaucrats had high, pointed Aragonese chairs in front of the dark, shining wood of the tables. Everyone was immaculately dressed, in lounge-suits, and a woman was there, laughing over the tips of her pink fingers.

I had come on a matter of buying some French francs—very difficult to get at that time —and had brought a special order with me. They handed it round the office and grumbled to each other. At last one of them said:

"I'll go and see whether it can be arranged, but I fear not," in a bored way, and slipped into an inner room.

I waited a long and boring time. The man did not come back.

"I'm afraid I can't wait much longer," I said at last. "I'm on business and I'm in a hurry."

I went to the inner door and opened it and went in. Two or three languid gentlemen were sitting round the table, smoking cigarettes. My order had fluttered to the ground and nobody noticed it.

I felt incredibly angry. This kind of thing sounds quite ordinary and usual to you. You find it in every office you go to. But for six months I had lived in the revolution, there was no bureaucracy and people went out straight ahead to do what they had to do, and everything had been different. In any of the locals this wouldn't have been tolerated.

I was back in democracy again!

"Would you mind going out, please, and staying outside of this private office?"

"No," I said. "You know I came with an order from the Minister of Propaganda. I'll ring him up now on this telephone and get it fixed, or you will."

The Minister of Propaganda was an old P.O.U.M. man, even though he had since backed out and joined the Liberals.

In the end, they were forced to telephone while I waited watching them. What was said to them over the wire I didn't catch, but something was certainly said. Afterwards they were sweet and kind, giving me an armchair and making conversation while they wrote out the slip for the cashier. I was haughty and wildly angry and disgusted. Because a Minister knew me personally! When I had come in my stained militia clothes that had not been good enough.

I was ushered out (with my francs) like a spring breeze.

Outside, I wandered about the lofty corridors. I looked at carvings and inscriptions and cursed the Anarchists for not having smashed the bourgeois power while they could have done so.

Their muddle-headedness had wrecked everything. Now we were forced to go shares in the
government with people like I had just seen—
the Liberal bourgeoisie.

Over another door I saw "Culture" painted
up. I remembered the Ventura Gassol was
Minister of that, and that we had known him
years before in Cuba. I went in to see him,
this time without red-tape for once, and the
room where he sat at a high reached desk
between two windows, facing a plain of parquet
flooring.

We chatted, interrupted by telephone-calls
and people coming to see him on various
businesses. To everyone he gave a brief and
courteous attention. He was off to Geneva. I
kept a warm impression of the shining, gleaming
dark room, and when I went out, thinking of
his manner, I said:

"At times, there is something to be said for a
visit to the bourgeoisie."

Gassol was intensely willing to help a friend.

Standing under the roofed arcades, talking to
a bullet-headed Anarchist later, I asked:

"Why did you put Juan P. Fabregas in as
Minister of Economy?"

"Because he's a good economist."

"I know. But he's not a revolutionary."

"Well, he's not in there to be what he wants
to be. He's there for us to pick his brains. If
he starts putting anything over on us, he'll go
out as quickly as he went in."

The Generality had other offices out facing the sea near the Columbus monument, and still others in the residential districts. One of these was the Ministry of Propaganda and there, from November until Moscow had the party put out of the Government, Max Petel and Paradell and I were sent as representatives of the Spanish Workers' Party. It was a big apartment building, clear and white inside and badly heated.

Of course it was the central goldmine for foreign journalists. After being there for a short while I thought very little of most of them and began to dislike them intensely.

The average journalist who came to Catalonia to report on the proceedings there had no particular convictions about the war and revolution, and didn't mind making this apparent. At a time when to us everything was life or death and black or white, this made us feel as though we were shaking hands with a fish. They were blasé, too, and all of them could have won the war for us ever so quickly, they said.

As a tall young man with a weak neck and fluffy moustache once remarked to me:

"I can't understand why they put so much party politics into this propaganda business. Why, if they put me on the job, I could sell Catalonia for about £400 a week."

There were also the kind of journalists who wanted to "see the front."

At first it had been fairly simple to take a car

and drive out to various points at the front. The war in its proper sense was not then under way and by taking sensible precautions the risk was not very great. Later it was different and we discouraged everybody. But journalists were always going and often getting hurt.

I remember three reporters from a French paper who insisted on having a car and touring the front. Only one of them came back alive.

At least one English reporter came once a day to interview Miravitlles, the Propaganda Minister. The reporter from the *Manchester Guardian*, who lived two or three worlds away from our tense excitement and reliefs, said to me of Miravitlles:

"What a delightful person he is. I think Miravitlles to be a man who can waste more time in a more charming manner than anyone I know."

In that he was completely wrong. Miravitlles never wasted any time. He was always working, and always appeared to be doing nothing.

He was a young man, sleek and dark and getting very plump. He had been the Secretary to the Anti-Fascist Militia Committee when it still existed. Now he sat at a desk and smiled with his hands clasped over his rising tummy. His smile was very sweet. Just then the telephone would ring. Riquener, tall, and looking as though he had just won a trophy at something, sped over the polished floor and announced:

o

"Paris on the 'phone."

Jaume Miravitlles put up both hands.

"Hush! Hush, everybody. Paris!"

He tiptoed to the gramophone and put it on gently in the middle of a record of Josephine Baker, as though it had been playing already, as though his gramophone were always nonchalantly playing airy Parisian nothings.

"Partir sur un batéau, tout blanc,
    Vers de nouveaux océans . . . "

When he had let the earphone rest near the turning disk for a moment, just to make quite sure, he lifted the mouthpiece and smiled sweetly into it as if he could be seen and lilted:

"Allo! Soy Miravitlles."

And the voice had a happy, singing tone as though he were certain it was a delightful thing to be.

He was nearly always gay, very diplomatic, generally ready to do what one wanted before one had even asked. He liked playing with a little red tape like a big child.

Working in the Ministry of Propaganda was more formal than anything I had done, and I chafed over it. I remember arriving the first day. I came as I was, with my rope-soled shoes and everything, only with my papers in a leather satchel. The cashier, who was a Liberal with a face like a block of ice, looked at me oddly. I wondered what was the matter. That evening one of the officials took me apart and politely, a little deprecatingly, clearing his throat:

"You—ah—you can't work here like that, I'm afraid."

"Like what?"

"In militia overalls. And those shoes. You see, we're receiving foreigners here all the time."

"And so we have to look like them? Although we're better? Although they've never found anything half as practical and neat and comfortable as us? Very well."

Benjamen Peret, too, the famous French poet, would not give up his overalls and startled the heads of Commissions by the disarming way in which he came to call. He had to come to see Miravitlles one day, who was impressed at the idea of meeting him.

Miravitlles was at his table, bent over some papers. Peret came to the door and opened it a little way, and put his pale, beaked head round it. Miravitlles looked up, but when he only saw a middle-aged worker with overalls and a bald head he looked down again and went on with what he was doing.

"There was a little slat loose in the floor boarding," he explained to me later, "and we had rung up to have someone come and mend it. I thought this must be the man. I asked him to come in, and wondered why he kept standing hesitating there. The more he hung about the more irritated I became.

"'What do you want?' I asked him finally.

"He gave me a little, shy bow.

"'I'm Benjamin Peret.'

"I had no breath left from surprise."

Miravitlles laughed and smoothed his flat black hair.

"And what did you think of him?" I asked.

"Oh, charming. How nice he is. Almost timid. After reading his books I was a little nervous of what he'd be like. I imagined him arriving here with the bleeding head of an arch-bishop under one arm and I don't know what under the other. And then when you meet him he's—well, a cross between a child and a bird."

It was very hard to remember to address people at the Generality as "ustedes." I remember rushing into the office of Catala—a short, broad man, with his hair carefully trained in wisps over a naked head—and calling him unguardedly "comrade," from habit, in our warm, casual way. He looked at me out of little round eyes like mulberries.

"Madam?" he asked. His politeness was icy.

In the room where we worked daily at issuing a propaganda bulletin there were only representatives of other workers parties and we were back on the usual footing. Most of the time we were reviewing the Press, reading and commenting the foreign newspapers which were at that time not allowed to circulate freely in Spain. Sometimes we wrote captions for photographs of Fascist atrocities, or the pictures of little dead children after the Madrid bombardments. An elderly woman journalist, who had come to interview us, burst into tears when she saw some of them. She hid her face in her hands.

"Oh, how can you? Sending out photographs of those dead children! It's too dreadful."

"We think so, too," I said. "Too dreadful that they should have been killed. But of course we didn't kill them."

She had long wisps of grey hair escaping from a beret. She looked at us through her thin knotted fingers.

"Brutes! How can you be such brutes? Think of all the women who are going to suffer when they see that, and think of *their* children."

"That would be the very best thing that could happen."

"Oh," she said, choking with rage. "How can you talk like that? Don't you realise that these are the sort of things which ought to be kept decently hidden?"

"Yes. While the *Daily Mail* continues to talk about the 'brave anti-red guards' serving their country (because I suppose even the British public would scarcely stand for 'brave Fascist'). Just up to us, I suppose, to keep all the things they do decently hidden."

But of course the English papers to which we sent the photos did not print them, on the sentimental account of a great many squeamish people who preferred to have their consciences spared. Only one eventually appeared—after an outcry by other sorts of readers—and that the

most romantic of them all, clouds of hair cover-
ing the blood and the unscarred face turned back
and up with a blank, a dark appeal in mouth
and eyes. I remember others, which you never
saw, with more surprised and dreadful expressions on the young faces stained and sometimes eyeless, and photographs of crowds of
people lying stiff and idle on the floors of refuges,
or in their beds, their hard outlines bulging the
sheets.

We were not long in the Generality. Things
were rapidly moving towards a different solution,
and the bourgeois-democrat element became
stronger every day. Nin was put out of the
Ministry of Justice, where he had installed the
revolutionary law-courts and set the first woman
judge on her circuit. No crimes had been
committed during his terms of office. It is
interesting to notice that during the early times
of a revolution common offences such as theft,
confidence tricks, and even the classic knifing
from jealousy totally disappear.

During the time when the crisis was coming to
a head we saw Nin every night at the newspaper
office.

"Will they manage to push us out?" we
invariably asked.

Nin shook his head.

"I don't think so. Companys said to-day
he'd resign the Presidency if the P.O.U.M.
went."

Since he had been in the Generality he had

always been too optimistic, perhaps too diplomatic.

"It's only a matter of hanging on now," he would say. "If we can hold out these next two or three days we'll weather it. It's bound to come to an end."

It was like a perpetually mattering wound. It healed in three days, and then followed a new, comatose period of fermenting under the skin, and then the trouble would begin again to come to another head.

In the end they made us go, thanks to the direct pressure exerted by Moscow. The road was safe for militarisation, then, away from any political control, though we had put up such a poor and muddled fight for the political control that the regular army would have come easily, anyway. The ministries were reshuffled. The Anarchists took a handsome handful, and the Stalinists came in under the thin cover of representing the U.G.T. Among other things, they had the Supplies Department.

On the very day that Comorera took it over there occurred the first shortage of bread in Catalonia, through mismanagement.

XVI

THE CHANGING ASPECT

(*Narrative by Mary Low*)

THE FIRST TAXIS HAD ALREADY CREPT BACK WEEKS ago. The F.A.I. seemed altogether to have forgotten the childish ferocity with which they had abolished the taxis in the first place. Now they were just as childishly proud of their new creation. Advertisements appeared on all the walls, showing the new cars, painted in the trades-union colours, sitting on a giant hand over the legend: "Our work." The colours were supposed to make everything all right.

Nearly all the men were wearing ties again. The workman's overalls had largely disappeared off the streets. More and more elegantly dressed women could be seen daily everywhere. When an Englishwoman, who had just arrived in Spain, walked into our local one day with two silver foxes draped over her shoulders, McNair of the I.L.P., who was then with us, felt obliged to say to her:

"You know, my dear, I don't think you ought to go walking about in Barcelona dressed quite like that."

To which the lady replied airily:

"Oh, it's all right. I saw several women with furs on as I came down the street."

Everyone had gradually given up wearing the militia costume, for now it had become the uniform of the regular army which was being formed and we had not come here to fight in any bourgeois regular army. Most of the International Column, who had taken Estrecho Quinto and Monte Aragon in days that already had their legend, were back in Barcelona doing political jobs or doing nothing because there was nothing they were freely allowed to do.

I remember seeing Calero come into the half-dark café on a winter afternoon. He wore the new winter military cap, and had stars on it to mark his grade, and we felt uncomfortable.

"Yes," he said, shaking our hands, "I have a command under Piquer in the new army."

"The officers get paid differently from the men, now, don't they?"

"Oh, I know it's anti-revolutionary, and all that, but how can a man stand up alone when they've imposed militarisation? We've got to fight the Fascists, anyway, and one must do it in the only way one's allowed to now."

We said nothing.

He leaned forward, begging us, with his warm, radiant smile, his hand against his left breast.

"You know—you do know, don't you?—that whatever happens I still have against my heart

that little image of a red world struck through
by lightning?"

"Oh, Calero, the sign of the Fourth International isn't kept hidden like that, in secret
against one's heart."

It was in the air. Everyone whose ideology
was not quite strong enough, whose character
was not quite staunch enough, began to let
themselves go the way the wind was blowing.
The regiments going down the streets marched
in perfect formation, one two, one two, the arms
swinging chest high and the hundreds of feet
striking down on the pavement with a single,
thunderous blow. The Catalan flag was carried
automatically with the red banners and the
black, there were less women mingled among
the men going to the front, there were no longer
dogs and cats following on the end of a string, or
perched on kit-bags. It was all as it should be,
and we stood more chance of winning the war
perhaps, but meanwhile the chance of winning
the revolution was growing gradually fainter.

It was when the big attack on Madrid began
that the first alarm signal of a Catalan nationalist
plot was sounded. The plot planned to leave the
rest of Spain to its fate and strike out for
autonomy, disregarding any responsibilities in-
curred outside of the Catalan frontiers. This was
a plot hatched by the bourgeoisie, of course.

As soon as the first rumours became public, the
F.A.I., which had seemed recently like a sleeping beast, roused itself and the next day arrested

200 of the Liberals. Everything was kept as quiet as possible, from the plot to the fate of the arrested men. But from what filtered through we gathered that some had been shot and others jailed. Everyone began to grow nervous and strained.

In order to show a truly splendid revolutionary spirit, as against all this, the Catalan workers poured down in quantities into the centre of the country, bringing reinforcements towards the central fronts. The best went, some of them veterans, and many others raw and untried, and whole picked regiments were flung one after the other into the breach. Durruti himself, the central force of the Anarchists in the north, had gone down there in person with his famous column. He died soon afterwards, hit by a sharp-shooter. The bullet went into the side of his body and reached the heart instantly.

It was like seeing a god or a statue killed, for already he unconsciously lived folded up in his legend. The Anarchists did everything they could to refuse this mortality. They embalmed the body, and put it on show, and even now one can look through an opening into the tombs and see their leader sleeping under glass. I couldn't help thinking, when we paraded at the funeral, that there was something very Spanish in the way the vestiges of religion clung to the revolution, and something comically so in the general impracticality of the whole proceedings. When we got to the cemetery, the tomb had been

carved out too small for the coffin and the pane
of glass too large for its frame, and everything
had to be done all over again. It poured with
rain, and the trees dripped on us, and the wind
howled through the black banners. The procession took eight hours getting through the
town to the cemetery, there were so many people.
They had brought him back from the Madrid
front so that the Anarchists could look at his
wounded body and decide by what treachery
he had been killed. It was too difficult for them
to admit that he had been shot like any ordinary
man.

The funeral itself was symptomatic of the
times. I stood sheltered from the wind in the
lea of a flag like a red sail, with John McNair,
and Breá, and Tusso (a member of our party
and the head of the Health Commission of
Catalonia), and Jordi Arquer and others, and
beside us a parallel line had formed. The
people in it carried huge wreaths of gold and
tawny flowers, and their striped flags licked sadly
out on the grey sky. On a silver streamer, I read:

"E.R.C. To our dear brother Durruti."

I laughed.

Arquer said:

"Dear brother, indeed! It's lucky for the
Republican Left that they're doing this at his
funeral and not anywhere else. He would have
rather had a machine-gun on them."

But the times were set towards reconciliation
and half measures. Some of us were beginning

already to be persecuted by the Stalinists for being too intransigent in the face of the new milk-and-water ways. Breá was arrested twice by them and his life put in danger. He was only rescued with difficulty. McNair, who is an excellent friend, a good diplomat, but no revolutionary, begged us almost with tears in his eyes not to answer the slanders they broadcast against us on the radio nightly, not to denounce their tactics in our Press. But how could we do otherwise, with the feeling of the revolution slipping like sand from under our feet every time a step was taken nearer to them? McNair and Brockway had worked for a common platform with the Communist Party in England, but on the real field of action things could not fail to be different.

The pressure going on against Madrid, and the sending of so many troops down to the centre made us feel the war more fully than before in Catalonia. The Generality set up an Office of Voluntary Works, and there people who could not leave jobs permanently came and offered their services for one day's work in each week. On that day they went away in carloads far outside the town and began digging fortifications. Preparations were made inside the town, too, which changed the aspect of Barcelona within a few days.

It was on coming out of a meeting of the Bolchevik-Leninist group that we had our first bombing practice. For some time before, big posters signed by Sandino, the non-party military technician within the Catalan Government, had appeared on the walls of houses and inside cafés, giving instructions of what to do in case of attack by air. A nice little opening paragraph asked everyone in friendly fashion to keep calm, and analysed the amount of danger they might expect:—a bomb of so many kilos could only destroy such-an-such an area, the surface of Barcelona was so-many times that area squared, therefore it would take so-many thousands of bombs dropped simultaneously to destroy the whole of Barcelona, therefore there was no need to alarm ourselves, etc. After that came the precise and succinct instructions, in Spanish and Catalan.

Soon after this, all the shop-keepers spent an afternoon out in the street on the pavement in front of their shops, unwinding long coils of coloured paper like curly snakes and sticking it in patterns over the windows. This was to avoid the glass flying if it broke. Some of the patterns were wonderfully pretty, and the dark winter streets were lightened as though towards spring by these perpetual trellisses which made one think of vines, and climbing roses and country inns.

Simultaneously with the paper, appeared great painted placards: "Refuge," and hands pointing to adjacent cellars. Little shuttered lanterns were suspended over these, with the light flung downwards, to be lighted when the street lamps went out.

It gave one an indescribably strange feeling to be closed within a town, and to see the signs of attack growing up round the walls. It was different at the front, where one went out to find the fighting.

We were in the cinema one night, between the hours of finishing work at the office at eight and starting work at the press at eleven. Nobody had any idea there was to be a practice. There were a lot of comfortably dressed folk, of the old former type who were beginning to put their heads out again and dare to show themselves, and young men of the "señorito" type with slicked hair and lounge suits and long slim hands, and numbers of workers, too. The film blacked out suddenly and a printed notice bobbed up:

"You are all asked to keep calm and follow the attendants down to the cellars. The film has been suspended by main force."

The lights went out, and then a few lanterns appeared.

Nobody thought of a practice, so there could only be one thing that the announcement could mean. It took us a minute to realise it. Then the excitement began.

I was a little nervous of what a latin-blooded crowd would do when put into a situation like this without warning, where there was no possibility of the immediate and dashing action at which they were so fine, nothing but the necessity for order, calm and patience. I was pleasantly surprised. Nearly everyone followed the attendants without pushing too hard, no one screamed, and only a few women of the prissy, dressy type wept bitterly, pressed against the arms of their men, but following where they were told all the same. Most of the workers looked at them with scorn. We decided, along with many of them, to go out into the streets and see what was really happening.

It was almost totally dark, and we stumbled on the uneven paving. Here and there, lights like dark blue smouldering jewels burned in the darkness. The refuge placards were faintly lighted, and a curious, uncanny whistling filled the air. At first I couldn't imagine what it was. Then, when we reached the Ramblas, we saw the Government cars touring slowly along, their lights lowered and glowing a deep orange and then changing to a purple that was nearly black, while all the time the strange zooming sound came out of special sirens attached to them. A man had his cigar lighted, and in the dark it seemed as bright as a torch. I saw an Assault Guard leap at him and smash it out of his hand, while the burning rain scattered everywhere around.

On all the street corners the militia-men were standing in orderly groups, guiding the people into the refuges with the minimum fuss. There was a lot of scampering, but no great signs of fright. We walked about looking up at the night sky. Bands of light broadened on it, lighting up the clouds and the deeps beyond, and then slid away in another direction. Sometimes they rayed out from all corners, crossing each other above our heads in an archway of swords.

It was not until the lights went up again half an hour later that we knew it had been a practice. The daily papers next day showed themselves very dissatisfied. People were not nearly frightened enough, they explained, and had showed a predilection for staying about in the streets to see what a bombardment looked like, instead of taking refuge. This made the task of the authorities much more difficult. We were severely trounced. A little later, when two Fascist 'planes were really sighted, the whole thing took place again, but this time, as people were convinced it was only a practice, they were more docile and incurious.

A little later the Fascists began tentative attacks from which they could hope obviously nothing but to unsettle the complacency of the Catalans on their own security. We had gone to dine at a café, and suddenly heard the unmistakable boom of big guns. It sounded oddly in the quiet, polished room, and the echo leaped back at us from the walls. We paid and went out at once.

In the street, there and then, I saw the revolutionary crowd in action. I was amazed at the speed, the efficiency with which the F.A.I. got their men under way, through the very elasticity of the organisation which so often stood them in

P

bad stead against a disciplined army on the field of combat. Every loud speaker in the town was talking. Instructions. Get your guns and man your lorries at once and go to the coast. Don't wait for further orders. Set off as soon as each lorry is filled.

A small crowd was stationed in the centre of the Ramblas. Ten minutes after the first alarm the lorries were roaring down on each side of the central avenue, the men standing up in them, packed tightly one against the other in their blanket coats, and the guns standing up with their pointed profiles above their backs. They cheered as they went by, waving wildly, and the dark mass rocked and swayed.

"F.A.I.! F.A.I.! C.N.T.!"

We roared back at them.

We hurried back to our local. We were more disciplined than they were, and the spontaneous action was not used in the same way. At the local, they were some time getting a lorry under way and having all the instructions given out and orders written, and in the end I was not sent. The coastal towns and villages belonged in large part to the P.O.U.M., and the local forces would be mobilising quickly there, so that there seemed less need to send so many of our people out from Barcelona, unless we heard that the attack was very severe. The leaders were on the radio all the time with the local branches, listening to what was happening, directing what was to be done.

For a long time I sat on a bench in the Ramblas, under the trees. All those who had not gone away in the lorries were parading up and down, and somehow the zest of the excitement was like new wine and we found ourselves talking endlessly and watching the cars rush by with tireless eyes. The patrols dispersed us every now and then, with orders to go home and clear the streets, but the little islands of people formed up again after their passage.

In the end, we went up to the Executive Committee and heard the messages that had come through. No, there had not been much damage done to the coast. No, nobody had managed to land from the ships. Yes, they were busy with fortifications and had already good results to show. After a while there seemed nothing more to do or see, and we went away to sleep.

That was the beginning. After that, from time to time the ship *Canarias*, and others, paid a small visit to the coast and let off long rumbling shots which brought the guard out running towards the shore defences. We became used to this. It seemed hardly dangerous, afterwards, no more than an undertone of war echoing a long way off the scene of action. Nevertheless, it showed that the net was closing round.

After this there were no more lights in the street at night, only the blue bulbs here and there to guide one along the main thoroughfares. But the cafés went on, behind the paper-striped windows, and the theatres and cinemas were the same.

A much better use might have been made of the films and of stage plays as means of propaganda in Spain. I remember some Americans coming to me once in distress and saying:

"You know some of the Anarchist represen-tatives at the Generality. Don't you think you could have a word with them about that film they're showing at the picture-house up the street?"

"What film is it?" I asked.

"Well, it's a silly darned thing about some college games, and the whole thing's so Fascist that all the Socialist Party in the States were having it banned from the local movies."

I went to some films of that kind, to see what happened. In general, the reaction in the audience was very sane. They laughed loudly and burst into ironic cheers when some passage full of bourgeois philosophy was presented to them. This comforted me considerably, but I still thought that a medium was being wasted.

I had a talk with an English camera-man who had come out there.

"In general, the pictures of the front aren't bad," he said. "They give a pretty good idea of how it happens, as much as one can expect to get from operating under danger while a battle is going on. And the scenery and so forth is well taken. The only trouble is, they stop at

that. The Fascists could do as much and get
as good results. They want to push the point
home more."

"I don't think more commentary is necessary,
if that's what you mean," I said. "Of course,
things have to be explained, but captions would
be better, so long as they were simple and sober,
because they take one less away from the real
moment than that voice."

"I didn't mean that," he said. He was a tall
grey man with a curious stutter. "I think the
pictures in themselves should be enough, if one
could only combine them from the human
interest angle. For instance, the other day I saw
some kids, hand in hand and quite alone, standing and looking at the ruins of their home, just
standing and looking, and of course there would
be no parents left to come back to. If we could
get things like that, to make people understand,
make them realise. . . ."

We went to two or three films done by the
Anarchists, and found them just as he had said.
It was curious, as I looked at them, in winter
now with the war become so much more deadly
and well-equipped, how the sight of the grass
and leaves waving below the noses of our guns
brought back the taste of the first moment when
we had walked up that hill towards the firing
line, with the prickles in our shoes. It seemed
as though so much had happened since that
landscape was real and breathing. It seemed
too far away.

We went to the theatre. Spanish acting is very poor, and their idea of play production primitive. The most revolutionary effort they had made so far was a staging of Romain Rolland's "Danton" in an arrangement and translation by our Gorkin (he is both a clever and a charming man) and excellently well done, but the spirit of the play infuriated us and we came away angry that the blunder had been made of showing it at that time. We needed to make the people believe so much in their spirit, then, and to stage a play in which they were shown deserting their leader in his hour of danger for the sake of a little bread! We stood outside the columned portico, in front of us a poster flapped in the rain—a foot in a Catalan sandal crushing a swastika with negligent, unquestioned strength.

We went also to some music halls, to see what they were like. They were always packed, generally filled to the brim with men from the militias back on leave, and surprisingly good. The audience joined in the fun like children, singing the songs in chorus and jumping up to help in the acrobatics. Suddenly some Aragonese singers came on to the stage in their curious costume— white knickerbockers and leggings overhung with a dark tunic, and handkerchiefs on their heads and a profound, pulsing silence stretched out over all the rows of listeners. They came to the front of the stage, with some women dressed in sober, circular shawls and full skirts, and began singing, and their strangely pitched voices threw the notes out in the vast hall in long, slow parabolas. It seemed as though an aim had been carefully taken for each, and they dropped towards us with a perfect, ripe descent. The mixture of the voices, one a semi-tone lower than the other and keeping exactly the pitch always, drew lovely geometric patterns in the air. The thrill of the responding audience touched me as I listened, and for long periods we sat there listening without speech. I felt full of a taut, excited pleasure. Afterwards they danced, and the enchantment sank to a more delicate key, but remained unbroken. The white legs moved in and out below the unmoving bodies, the feet still following an unanswerable pattern in which every line was unexpected and yet inevitable.

I thought this Aragonese art grave and beautiful.

There was one important thing more, in the way of entertainments, and that was the bull-fight. Great numbers of the matadors were on the anti-Fascist side, and many of them had joined the militias and gone to the front. The fights continued to be given on Sundays, with a socialisation of the profits, the Anarchists and the Communists sharing out the places on the bull-ring committees between them. The crowd were very numerous at these shows, and were as critical and appreciative as ever.

There was a certain amount of opposition, however.

A fair Catalan boy, with blue fierce eyes, said to me, one day while I stood reading a poster about the next appearance of the Niño de la Estrella in Barcelona:

"That's one thing which the triumphant revolution will have to do away with."

"Bull-fighting?"

"Yes. That and the lottery." He nodded sagely at me. "You're an international, perhaps you don't know. But those two things are the curse of Spain."

He showed me various newspapers on a stand which we passed which ran campaigns against them.

"You see? It's not a fad. The serious revolutionaries think like me. Those things are part of Spain's backwardness."

"You intend to root them out, do you? Well, from what I can see of it, you've got a long job before you. Still," I said, smiling a little, "there's always to-morrow, isn't there? 'Mañana.'"

He threw back his head and laughed, with sudden boyish exuberance.

"That! oh, 'mañana,' that's a Spanish curse, too, perhaps worse than the bulls and the lottery. . . ."

It was a word which worried the internationals to the verge of distraction.

"Everything in this country's governed by that dreadful word," a German comrade said to me once, with a heavy groan. "If they used it even once in Germany in circumstances like these, it'ud be all up with their chances. How fortunate that the enemy are Spanish, too—so much more Spanish, even, than we are here."

XVII

THE JOURNEY BACK

(*Narrative by Mary Low*)

THERE WAS LITTLE MORE TO KEEP US IN BARCELONA after January. The militias were over, with the coming of militarisation. The Generality was done for, as far as we were concerned. There remained the war to be won, certainly, but it was the revolution in which we were interested. For the time being it seemed to have gone into cold storage.

We were considerably saddened by saying good-bye. Molins, a likeable chap because of his enthusiasm, and Gorkin, the heads of the Press, tried their best to induce us to stay. We had worked with them with such great good cheer and high hopes. There were many others we were unhappy to leave.

On the last night of all we went up into the hills behind Barcelona to the house where some of the comrades lived. It was quiet there, with scarcely a building, except here and there a deserted house which had once belonged to some wealthy Fascist family. Sometimes there were Fascists lurking in the gardens, and when they tried to escape there was shooting in the valley. But the shots sounded so desolate and far away in the darkness that they seemed almost natural, like an echo, native to the evening.

On that last night we had gathered together there all those people who (political considerations for once set aside) we had liked best during our six months in Spain. That is to say, those who were still alive. We all sat slouching near one another in wide chairs, guessing each other's profile a little here and there by the first rays of a moon which was struggling up behind the hollow of the hill. Somebody spoke a poem in a deep, soft voice. As my eyes grew used to the darkness, I saw Serna leaning fatly on his stick, his hair like a rich crinkly bush above his brow, and Lafargue with his heavy, pale head like a Roman bust come down from its stand, McNair with his nose and lower lip stuck well forward, Lou Lichfield lighting a cigarette with patient gestures from a stub of smouldering wick which lighted the lower part of his face and the mouth that resembled Oscar Wilde's. Lili, who was lovely and intelligent, and tired with the effort to teach Spanish women daily to be free and strong, lay stretched out flat on a sofa.

"Sometimes I think they'll understand," she said, "and sometimes I think—well, it must be hopeless, like filling a tank with a thimble. There's so little one person can do."

"It all seems like that when I look back on my work here," I said. "Like the scratching of mice. But the best of all is that we know it must count, after all, a kind of collectivised effort which leads to something, since the revolution does not rely upon the workings of a single man."

McNair had arrived later than the others. The house was a long way away, and he had had to come in a taxi and didn't speak Spanish. It seemed the middle of the night when I opened the door in answer to his ring.

He was on the doorstep, and had his arm round the chauffeur.

"This is a splendid chap," he said. "He's really my friend. I wish you'd tell him so, I can only make him understand by signs. But I didn't know where the place was, and couldn't tell him, but he wouldn't leave me and we've been muddling our way round for hours in the dark here. He really is a splendid chap."

I told him, and he grinned and patted McNair on the back.

I asked him if he would come back there at four o'clock.

"You're our only hope between now and the early train," I said, "and there's no telephone. So you mustn't let us miss it."

"Oh, no, he won't," McNair said. "He refused to let me down."

He didn't let us down either. Just before four

he was there, sounding the hooter until we came and entered the taxi.

Since the revolution nearly everyone is extraordinarily honest in Spain. The only thing they ever seem to steal at all are revolvers, and that is pardonable, for firearms are so short and precious. They come on time to appointments, which they never used to before. I always left my door unlocked, sometimes with coins on the table, and nothing was ever taken.

Once in the very early morning I had got up and was walking down the Ramblas alone when it was still under morning mist. There was almost no one there. I had a hole in my pocket and had forgotten about it, and transferred some money to it while I was walking. There were leaves on the ground which had not yet been brushed away, and I did not hear the chink of it falling.

Somebody yelled out behind me:

"Hi! Hi! Wait a minute."

I had seen a group of two or three militiamen, sauntering idly, and had passed them almost without noticing. Now I thought, they're only trying to get into conversation, they so often called after anything in a skirt, and I paid no attention.

They called out several times more, without making me turn. Then I heard them running behind me on their light shoes. I stopped and turned round.

One of the boys was quite flushed and panting.

"Here you are," he said. "You dropped this.
You weren't in much of a hurry to get it back,
were you?"

There were several quite big coins. No one
had been about. The pay of a militia-man is
very small.

The Anarchists were doing a lot, too, in their
new campaign for a simple life of natural
sobriety.

It was dark and damp when we reached the
station to catch the market train that morning
at half-past four. We had snatched a coffee on
the way at a stall where some of the Republican
Guard were standing, their faces half wrapped
in the sleepy folds of their cloaks, and leaning
negligently on their guns. In the station, old
women with handkerchiefs over their heads
were waiting patiently in rows, their baskets
laid on the concrete paving at their sides, and the
bright fruit and green leaves overflowed under
the guttering lights of the hall.

The train was a local one, and we sat between
the market women on the slatted bench watching
the last outlines of Barcelona slip slowly away.
I leaned out of the window in the freshness and
the dark. I looked back. In spite of everything, of all our conclusions, the regret came up
bitter in my mouth and I knew then that we
were leaving the centre pivot of the world.

We slept in spasms. The train jolted to a halt
through all those villages which we had passed
in coming here last summer, but they seemed

different now, the walls sodden under the rain,
their gay whiteness discoloured and sad, and all
the time I kept thinking how difficult now it
would be to adjust one's self again to the bourgeois world. All kinds of things I had taken for
granted, or not noticed at all, seemed suddenly
dear, and I felt out gropingly towards the days
that were coming as though I had forgotten the
shape of that life.

It was Port Bou again. We got off the train
with our knapsacks on our backs, and stood
waiting to be seen by the red customs guard.
When we came to the counter, and slung our
packs down on to it, the man looked up at
us with a smile that crinkled up all the long
tired wrinkles in his face like parchment, and
asked:

"Going back again now, comrades? Well, I
wish you luck."

"Thanks," we said.

"Tell them about us over there," he said, and
he raised his fist slowly above the shoulder. We
answered it. I felt curiously moved to stand like
this for the last time among workers who were
freely my comrades, and salute, and the moment
seemed to stand still and run back endless
stretches into the past behind me.

There was a little examination room which
came next. They sent us in, one by one, into
separate compartment for the men and the
women, to search our clothes. I had thought
it would be only a nominal search, and I had

strapped my revolver—which I didn't want to give up—into a belt below my dress.

I was wrong. There were two thin, strong women in the room, dressed in black, and they took me by the arms, and one of them said:

"You will excuse us, comrade, won't you? But this absolutely has to be done. It isn't that we don't trust you, but we must do it, that's all."

I felt instantly ashamed, and pulled out the revolver.

"Here. I suppose you'd better take it. It's like pulling out my front teeth to give it up, though."

"You'd have had awful trouble if it had been found on you in France."

"I suppose so."

I felt very morose. They touched me all over and looked in my handbag. They read everything, but there was nothing they could object to. Afterwards I put on my coat again, and one of them said:

"I'll come over with you to the guard-room and we'll see what can be done about the revolver."

As we went out of the room together another woman, rather elderly came in. The examiner felt her, and instantly pulled out a long black rosary from round her neck.

"Why, whatever are you doing with that?" she cried. She seemed to think that it was rather funny than offensive. The woman murmured something, and the girl took the rosary out into the court of the customs room where all the men were gathered round, and shook it out and then called:

"Just look what I've taken on somebody!"

They looked, and when they saw that it was an old, poor woman who had been caught with it, most of them laughed with a great deal of good humour. One of them threw it away with casual cheerfulness.

"Teach her something gayer than that," he called out.

I was reminded of Grossi, and his story about the local priest at Lesiñena.

Grossi, whom we had known on the Aragon front—author, captain and miner—came from the Asturias and was a hundred per cent a working man. With that, he was very far from being the intellectualised type of worker who has been to Russia and all the rest, and in spite of his undeniable success as a writer he continued to be a worker unadorned. If you had ever heard him laugh, you would know what sort of a man he was, cut all of one piece.

He had already taken Lesiñena several days ago, so he told us then, and still hadn't managed to lay hands on the priest.

"How could we be expected to find him," he asked us, "when the town committee was keeping him in hiding? Well, we found out that he apparently wasn't a bad sort of chap, this priest. The only sins he seems to have committed was that his nephew looked a bit too much like him and that he was rather fond of the bottle. However, as you know, fornication is no sin to us, and as he kept on repeating that he was "only a worker, too, a humble worker at God's tasks," and as all the workers are presenting their vindications now, well," said Grossi, finally, "that little chap of a priest has been allowed to go free and given an unlimited holiday."

When I got to the guard-room with the woman examiner we found two or three comrades gathered round, taking up a little pale sunshine that was coming in through the window.

"This comrade had a revolver on her that she wanted to take into France."

"I'm afraid you can't do that, comrade," one of the men said.

"What a marvellous weapon."

It was. They stood round and looked at it admiringly. It was a 1936 Colt. I felt I couldn't bear parting with it.

"I'll tell you what you can do, though. You can give it as a present to someone, and that's the next best thing to keeping it for yourself. Come on, anyone you like? Name the chap, and we'll see that he gets it safely. Or would you rather have us put it in the safe here, with your name on a label, and kept, and then you can have it again if you come back?"

"I mightn't be coming back," I said. "Give it to comrade Fort for me."

I thought how different was the spirit of all

this from the average customs. We stayed talking, I leaning against the lintel, chatting about the revolution.

Then the train came in, and we went to France.

There was Cerbere again, as dirty and tired as I remembered it, but now a fine rain was falling. We took refuge in a café after the customs had finished with us, and were amazed at how high the prices seemed to be. It was all different. It was all sadder. We got up again and shouldered our packs and went out and began to stroll about dismally in the strip of road under the rain.

Perhaps if one could get to the beach by some short cut instead of going all that way round the main street it might be worth it. I looked around for someone to ask.

Just then a portly figure surged up. We waited till he came a little nearer, then I went forward to meet him. He was wearing a French army officer's uniform, and looked kind and rubicund. He wheezed a little. His belt's too tight, I thought. I felt indulgently towards him, glad to have someone at least to talk to in this stale landscape with its dreary, perling rain.

"*Dis-donc, camarade,*" said I, grabbing him carelessly by the arm, "*est-ce que tu peux me dire——*"

He shook me off wrathfully. The height to which he suddenly towered was alarming.

"I beg your pardon, Madame."

Q*

I sighed. I had forgotten. It had begun again.

The next day we were in Paris, and everything was over, even to the last mistakes of forgetting that we were ladies and gentlemen and the lower classes.

CHAPTER XVIII

CONCLUSION

(By Juan Breá)

THE JOURNEY WAS OVER, BUT NOT THE SITUATION in Spain, which needs a word of comment and analysis to put a full stop to this book. There are certain conclusions to be drawn which should dig deeper than passing personal impressions. There is also a forecast to be drawn up for the future.

In many ways, the Spanish situation has certain analogies with the Russian. The outbreak of both those revolutions came as an immense surprise to the bourgeoisie, who, due to their ignorance of the revolutionary dialectics of history, had their heads busily turned away in another direction at the time, sniffing up a false scent and awaiting events anywhere but there. They had never shown any surprise at the economic backwardness of Russia or Spain, and according to their concepts, political development could scarcely reach further than economical development. The surprise was therefore general, that an economically backward country should turn out after all to have pursued its political advancement.

The capitalist diagnosis was that the Spanish proletariat had rushed on to something for which they were not ripe. This false impression, and the surprise, gave the bourgeoisie another disagreeable proof that things were going contrary to their convenient principle that "nature makes no leaps and bounds."

The same astonishment cropped up again:

"Oh, here's the revolution in Russia when we were expecting it in Germany!

"Oh, revolution in Spain when we thought it would be in France."

The idea that Spain was safe from the proletarian revolution of course sprang from the fact that the bourgeois revolution had not yet occurred there. In Spain, the feudal system has had a long reign because, by the time the bourgeoisie in the rest of Europe were coming into full flower, Spanish economy had reached its greatest decadence. Already the colonies had either disappeared or were on the point of slipping away. The Spanish bourgeoisie was unable to become a revolutionary class before the springing up of imperialism irrevocably condemned it as such. From being too retarded, the bourgeois revolution was never to come to a head, its furthest development was merely to enter into certain contradictions with the still existing feudalism.

The proletariat therefore remained the only revolutionary class. It had reached a certain development, and it was impossible to reconcile its interests with those of other classes. As a genuinely revolutionary force it was already turning to its own advantage the friction between the bourgeoisie and feudalism. The result of this was inevitably that the capitalist classes began to look upon feudalism less as a foe than something to be turned to account as an ally in the struggle against the common foe—the proletariat.

All this had happened under the monarchy, and the stage was now set for the Republic.

The Republic was no more than an electoral success. In ridding themselves of the more outward trappings of feudalism, the bourgeoisie canvassed the vote of the proletariat and the peasantry by making three promises. These promises concerned the church, the land and the army; and the bourgeoisie, although they came into their own politically, were able to keep none of them. If anything were still needed to show the complete liquidation of the bourgeoisie as a revolutionary force, their failure to solve these problems offers a final and shining proof.

The problems were prickly. In the first place, the Republic found itself unable to do without the clergy which it had so glibly promised to eliminate. If it had put out the clergy it would have had to close down the schools. Practically all teaching was in the hands of religious orders, and they had deeply infiltrated themselves besides into the economy of the country, holding large shares everywhere and owning the heaviest percentage of interests in the railways. Therefore, in putting them out, the Republic would have touched private property; and Spain was not in the same case as France, where the bourgeoisie was sufficiently devoted to be able to attack feudal property without endangering private property in general. For this reason, every form of private property, even feudal property, was taboo to the Spanish Republic. However, obliged to do something to save its face, the Republic dissolved the Jesuit orders. That was as far as it dealt with the clergy.

As to the agrarian problem, even fewer measures were taken. The wealth of the country was largely in the fields, and the poorest and most hard-ridden workers were there, too. It was their help which had so powerfully backed the republicans at the elections, on the promise of more tolerable conditions of life. But after all, once in and secure, the republicans were able to reflect at leisure that it would be idle to put the riches of country up against them, as personified by the big land-owners who, of course, had every interest in keeping things as they were. Spain depends economically on the land, because, except in Catalonia, industry is slight. The sole solution, therefore, offered by the Republic was the now comically famous Agrarian Reform Plan which never got beyond the pigeon-holes of the Ministry of Agriculture.

The army was the most ticklish subject of the lot. To understand the history of Spain it is first of all necessary to understand what its army means, and the huge part it has always played.

The Republic could not even attempt to touch the army, when it came to the point. The army did not mean, for well-born Spanish families, one of half a dozen acceptable and respectable careers, as it does in other European countries. It meant *The* career, the only real career, unless one went into the church, and the result of this was that there was one officer to every six men. They had successively arranged the destinies of the country and its ruin. The Spanish colonial system had been that of military governor-generals, sent out to each colony, who sucked the country dry for their own personal convenience at no profit to Spain, and in this way gradually lost every land which they had subjected. As there was a general for every colony, when the colonies were lost and the generals came back home, each of them had to be given a town to govern instead. So a system grew up in which every little district had its general. Apart from that, the Army had political pretensions, arranged the ruling of the country to suit its own taste by such methods as military coups, rebellions, coups d'états, and other measures of the same kind.

The cream of the whole military corps, from a point of view of the purest reaction, was the famous Civil Guard. The Republic, when it was brought about, was careful above all not to attack this body. The republicans were even careful to leave San Jurjo at the head of the Guard in spite of the part he had played and what he represented.

The Republic having shown its feet of clay on that matter, as on all the others, a reaction inevitably set in. The pendulum swung back, and at the next elections it was a group much further to the right who came to power, although still holding up a mask of democracy over the growing signs of Fascism. But from that to an open declaration could not be a long step. The Left grew restless and aware of the danger, and then we have at last the People's Front constituted as a means for getting a majority at the polls.

The electoral success of the People's Front was like a tide breaking all barriers. And here the Spanish side of the story comes into play. The army was taken by surprise and felt itself menaced by this success and decided once more to change things by a characteristic intervention. This was on the 19th July, 1936. For once the army had miscalculated. Hitherto it had only been used to dealing with the Court, or Liberal ministers, easy pawns to pick up and move here and there according to the necessities of the game. But this time the proletariat had entered the contest, and in no mean manner.

The results, as we have seen, were totally unexpected by the bourgeoisie.

"The Spanish proletariat is not ripe for the revolution" is one of the great catchwords, and they bolster it up by saying that the revolution would not have come if Fascist provocation had not precipitated it. The fact that Fascism provoked it does not, however, go to show that the proletariat were neither ripe nor sufficiently class conscious. They were, and to prove it I would point out that in Barcelona, Valencia and Madrid, it was not the legally constituted Government which crushed the Fascist rising, but the people themselves.

What that business does go to prove is the political corruption which exists in some of the groups which lead the proletariat. Throughout this book I have shown the ideological confusion reigning among the Anarchists, who threw away the power when it fell into their hands because their principles were against taking it. As to those affiliated to the Third International, the counter-revolutionary rôle they have played in Spain is only too well known. It comes as a consequence of Russian nationalism, and in a moment I will deal with the part Russia has played in the Spanish situation and with all its disastrous results. Add to this the old tradition of democracy disguised as trade union and political reformism, and you will see why the revolution had to wait on a Fascist provocation. All these factors explain the absence to-day of a workers' Government and the deeply serious menace which that absence is to the revolution.

It is now necessary to go more carefully into Russia's attitude towards the Spanish revolution and the reasons which determined it. This is bound up with the international situation, one side of which licked its lips openly over the conflict while the other viewed it as a considerable annoyance. The two sides, of course, were Rome and Berlin versus France and England. Hitler and Mussolini saw in all that a pleasant way of getting their feet into Spain and enlarging their scope, while France and England could only see that they might be drawn into a war in which they had nothing to gain and absolutely everything to lose.

The Russian position is rather different from either of these.

From its centrist position, the Stalinist Government is naturally placed outside the course of the international revolution. It is impossible for the U.S.S.R. to foresee revolutionary events. The U.S.S.R. is no longer in touch and in line, and when revolutionary phenomena occur it is always taken by surprise. Then we see the Soviet Government balancing from side to side, seeking by swinging about to find the right and opportune reaction. As it has not foreseen the revolutionary event, it fails to understand it. It feels from right to left and goes from Herod to Pilate.

Look at the first attitude of the Soviet Union towards the Spanish revolution. When the Fascist rising broke out on July 19th, 1936, and the huge revolutionary tide replied to it by washing down over the country, Stalinist bureaucracy had seen nothing and therefore was prepared to do nothing. It took refuge in a prudent policy of a spectator to the right. It did nothing at all until Italy and Germany had done so much that a Fascist triumph seemed immanent. Franco was already at the gates of Madrid before the U.S.S.R. had decided on an active attitude. The realisation of what a real danger a Fascist Spain would be to its own interests finally woke it up. A Fascist Spain on one side of France, and Germany and Italy on the other would of course speedily mean a Fascist France. The Soviet Union would then lose its only European ally.

The time had come for action. The Soviet Government decided to rush into the breach at last. However, it was to do so on its own terms.

The terms sprang from the nationalist policy of Stalin. Since he had become a member of the "gang of thieves" at Geneva he was tied up to France and in the throes of a long flirtation with England. Both these countries were against Franco because they have nothing to gain from a Fascist Spain. As they have still less to gain from Communism, the formula of a Spanish democratic republic struck them as the happy medium, and it was to this formula which Stalin gave his adhesion.

Meanwhile, we in Spain had forgotten all about the Spanish democratic republic for at least three months. We had been making and living the revolution, especially in Catalonia, the industrial heart of Spain, where the Anarchists are in the majority and do not need to wait on Moscow. Elsewhere the revolution had also frankly broken out. The Government at Madrid was a coalition between the Communists and the petty bourgeoisie, but no one doubted that we were all heading for the dictatorship of the proletariat.

I can well remember the first reappearance of the words: "Spanish democratic republic." They came with the first coughing of the first Russian gun. There was surprise and indignation at first, but afterwards people knuckled under because they felt that they had to have the arms. It was then that things went wrong, to the tune of "win the war first and make the revolution afterwards."

This is where we meet once again with the old Stalinist policy of "deceiving the bourgeoisie." When Stalin openly gave up leaning for support on the international working class and decided to base his policy on diplomacy, which meant joining the League of Nations, he whispered slyly into the ear of the proletariat:—

"That's to deceive the bourgeoisie."

To-day, after telling the Spanish worker to give up the revolution in favour of the Spanish democratic republic, he is busy whispering to them the same consolation.

But both the international bourgeoisie and

the Spanish bourgeoisie are quite wary. They are willing that Russia should help, but want to know exactly with what intentions. They want guarantees that it was really for the capitalist democratic republic. We all know that there is only one guarantee for a State and that is its army. At the time when the Soviet Union decided to help, the people's militias were the fighting force, an absolutely revolutionary body which could offer no guarantee for a capitalist republic.

Stalinism decided to change all that.

I am far from wanting to maintain that the militias were perfect and that their reform was not called for: they were a spontaneous army of the people, and had all the faults which that condition is heir to. There was no discipline, very little control, and a complete lack of cohesion. Every political party had its own little army and did as it pleased. People came and went on leave without notifying the responsible parties, and regiments moved about in the most unexpected way. I well remember, at the taking of Estrecho Quinto on the Aragon front, that an Anarchist column was not pleased at having been asked to take part in a preliminary attack which failed, and, becoming annoyed, they took their cannon and moved further off. Afterwards they were still more annoyed at not having been present for the victory.

As time went on it became more and more urgent to organise an army. The enemy had a real army, and the only thing which can stop a real army is another real army. There are two ways of making it: by forming a red army, or by forming a bourgeois army.

It was impossible to make the red army in Spain at the time. The revolution was not far enough advanced to possess its own Government, unadmixed by any bourgeois elements, which, together with its army, would be the expression of its interests. On the other hand, it was not so backward that the formation of a regular bourgeois army would be natural. That would have been the very proof that the people totally lacked influence.

The only thing to do was to seek a middle means, to carry on with until the revolutionary situation should become ripe enough for a red army. A formula was found which should have been temporarily adopted. The P.O.U.M. which is after all a revolutionary party, put forward the idea. It proposed the acceptance of the unified command and the imposition of discipline as in a regular army, but meant to keep the army under the people's control by having political delegates sent to it from the different parties. In this way the conquests of the revolution would have been guaranteed.

However, the Stalinists had no intention of taking into consideration these conquests, or paving in this way the road for a future red army. They had the arms and meant to dictate the terms. They blackmailed the Anarchists, holding out on the armaments question until the P.O.U.M. formula was rejected. To-day, by gentle degrees, the whole fighting force is passing into a regular army in the control of the republican capitalist Government.

When the army has become perfectly bourgeois, a new situation will arise. Indeed, this is so near upon us now that the first rumours are already making themselves heard in the Press. The moment will come when two regular bourgeois armies will find themselves face to face and suddenly realise that their reason for fighting each other has ceased to exist.

A pact will follow. This pact may prove itself to be the curious final solution offered by Stalinism to save Spain. From the beginning of the revolution we have not seen a single revolutionary measure proposed by Stalinism. While the P.O.U.M. and the Anarchists had adopted such slogans as: "For a Junta of Workers, Peasants and Militia-men", and "Divide the Land", and others of a more or less revolutionary nature, the sole solution offered by the official Communist Party was the elimination of Trotskyism. This was announced plainly from the very beginning. The board was swept clean of every revolutionary slogan to give way to:— "The condition for victory over Franco is the crushing of Trotskyism." (Agenda of the Presidium of the Communist International in November.)

After having said all this, and insisted so

much on the Stalinist influence in Spain, I must point out that the failure of the Spanish revolution should not be laid at the door of Stalinist bureaucracy. It would be childish to throw the blame there when we have known so long what a counter-revolutionary part Russia and her acolytes have been playing in all countries. Forewarned is forearmed. The responsibility must lie with those revolutionary parties in Spain who know Stalinism for what it is. I mean the P.O.U.M. and Anarchists, and the Anarcho-Syndicalists.

The one attitude which they should have taken, and failed to, should have been based on a realisation of Russia's motives and her interests. Whether we consider it under either of two heads the equation works out the same in the end.

In the first place, if Russia is still a proletarian State there are no complications. As a proletarian State, she obviously must not only support democracy against Fascism but must go further and support Communism against Fascism. If Communism and Fascism were put face to face in Spain, eliminating the possibility of a democratic medium, she would be forced in spite of herself to give her preference to Communism as a policy of the lesser evil. Apart from everything else, her prestige would demand it in order to keep up her professed attitude.

Therefore, the only thing to do is to oppose Communism to Fascism in Spain.

On the other hand, let us suppose that Russia is no longer a proletarian State but is making her first steps towards capitalism. She therefore has no class interests in the struggle, but her national interests remain just as strong as ever and would force her to go to any lengths to prevent the occupation of Spain by Germany and Italy. Naturally she would stick out for the formula of the democratic republic as long as possible, even to threats and armament blackmail in the hopes of bluffing her way through. But if her hand was forced, the interests of her own self-protection would force her to support even Communism against Fascism, in spite of her definite antagonism to the Socialist revolution.

Therefore, under the second head as under the first, the answer to the solution is the same: oppose Communism to Fascism in Spain. We are sure of help.[1] If Communism triumphs in Spain, Russia will accept it as the best of a bad case, in order to maintain her mask as a proletarian state. Actually, of course, a communist Spain would be the first to rise up and unmask Russia. Russia knows this, and the whole contradiction of her policy is resumed in the fact that, in spite of this knowledge, she is forced to help Communism because her national interests are at stake on the question of Fascism.

The Anarchists have not understood this and have allowed themselves to be bluffed.

How wrong they are is still another question.

[1] In our opinion, the Soviet Union at the present time is no longer a proletarian state, and not yet a capitalist one. Of course, this makes no difference to the answer to the above equation."—M.L.—J.B.

One must realise that, whatever happens, the idea of democracy in Spain, once this civil war is over, is pure Utopia. The country will be in far too dismembered a state, economically, to admit of anything but a dictatorship. Whether this dictatorship be Fascist, bourgeois, or proletarian, only the outcome of the present struggle can decide, but a dictatorship of some sort it will be. It is idle to talk of democracy.

The reign of the People's Front is over. If it has known success in France, in holding back the coming of Fascism, it might equally have had such a success in Germany in stopping Hitler's rise to power, but in any case it should have been a Common Front—that is to say an alliance of the proletariat without an amalgamation of programme. But the Spanish case is not the French or the German case. There will be little left of Spanish economy when the war is over, and what remains will need sticking together with something considerably stronger than the paste of democracy.

To sum up, the only prospect offered by Stalinism in Spain is to win the war and to lose the revolution. We believe that if the revolution is lost, the war can only with very difficulty be won, and after all, for what? The people at least will have nothing, with even the breath of democracy blown away.